MW00467330

PHENOMENOLOGY OF CHICANA
EXPERIENCE AND IDENTITY

New Critical Theory
General Editors:
Patricia Huntington and Martin Beck Matuštík

The aim of *New Critical Theory* is to broaden the scope of critical theory beyond its two predominant strains, one generated by the research program of Jürgen Habermas and his students, the other by postmodern cultural studies. The series reinvigorates early critical theory—as developed by Theodor Adorno, Herbert Marcuse, Walter Benjamin, and others—but from more decisive post-colonial and post-patriarchal vantage points. *New Critical Theory* represents theoretical and activist concerns about class, gender, and race, seeking to learn from as well as nourish social liberation movements.

Phenomenology of Chicana Experience and Identity: Communication and Transformation in Praxis
by Jacqueline M. Martinez

The Radical Project: Sartrean Investigations
by Bill Martin

PHENOMENOLOGY OF CHICANA EXPERIENCE AND IDENTITY

Communication and Transformation in Praxis

JACQUELINE M. MARTINEZ

ROWMAN & LITTLEFIELD PUBLISHERS, INC.
Lanham • Boulder • New York • Oxford

ROWMAN & LITTLEFIELD PUBLISHERS, INC.

Published in the United States of America
by Rowman & Littlefield Publishers, Inc.
4720 Boston Way, Lanham, Maryland 20706
http://www.rowmanlittlefield.com

12 Hid's Copse Road
Comnor Hill, Oxford OX2 9JJ, England

Copyright © 2000 by Rowman & Littlefield Publishers, Inc.

All rights reserved. No part of this publication may be reproduced,
stored in a retrieval system, or transmitted in any form or by any
means, electronic, mechanical, photocopying, recording, or otherwise,
without the prior permission of the publisher.

British Library Cataloguing in Publication Information Available

Library of Congress Cataloging-in-Publication Data

Martinez, Jacqueline M., 1961–
    Phenomenology of Chicana experience and identity : communication and
transformation in Praxis / Jacqueline M. Martinez.
        p. cm. — (New critical theory)
    Includes bibliographical references and index.
    ISBN 0-7425-0700-9 — ISBN 0-7425-0701-7 (pbk.)
        1. American literature—Mexican American authors—History and
criticism—Theory, etc. 2. American literature—Women authors—History
and criticism—Theory, etc. 3. Mexican American women—Intellectual
life. 4. Feminism and literature—United States. 5. Women and literature
—United States. 6. Mexican Americans—Communication. 7. Feminist
theory. I. Title. II. Series.

PS153.M4 M37 2000
810.9'9287'0896872—dc21   00-024819

Printed in the United States of America

⊗™ The paper used in this publication meets the minimum requirements of
American National Standard for Information Sciences—Permanence of Paper
for Printed Library Materials, ANSI/NISO Z39.48-1992.

this book is
lovingly and gratefully dedicated to

my parents

Octavio Martinez   Patricia C. (Martinez) Foster

and grandparents

Cruz Martinez   Ardelta Wood
Octavio Tergo Martinez   Luther L. Wood

to whom I owe everything

CONTENTS

PREFACE

This book is about Chicana experience and identity. I have written it in large part for Chicanas, although I am certain that the issues and concerns addressed here are relevant for a wider audience as well. I am thinking specifically about other women of color, people of color generally, and all of those interested in transforming discriminatory and oppressive conditions into ones that make liberation and human freedom facts of individual and collective experience and not just ideology or hyperbole. It is this concern for the difference between freedom as a fact of human experience and mere assertions about it that define much of my interest in the work presented here. Within certain academic circles it is commonplace to talk about liberation, transformation, and tearing down the circumstances and structures that create oppressions of all sorts. Yet, even among the best of this work, there is an inevitable gap between the words spoken or written and the fact of lived experience. Given even the most eloquent of written texts or engaged dialogue, the fact of human freedom and liberation achieved in the actual experience of persons often remains in question. In other words, those of us who address issues of liberation and transformation of oppressive social and cultural conditions can never really be certain when and under what circumstances our efforts actually have something of the effect on ourselves and the community that we hope they will.

This is where my use of phenomenology comes in. Both a theoretical perspective concerning the nature of human existence and an applied research procedure for explicating features of human existence, phenomenology offers a rich field of discourse and practice from which to consider the issues addressed here. As a theoretical perspective, phenomenology focuses our attention on the life world and the lived experience of persons. Phenomenology takes this focus because it recognizes the inherent interrelatedness of human conscious experience and the fact of our locatedness in time, place, history, and culture. What I come to experience at any given moment in my life is not merely idiosyncratic—reducible to a peculiarity of my uniqueness. And neither can what I experience be determined solely by facts of my culture, community, time, or place. Rather, what I come to experience at any given moment is a dynamic interrelation between what my culture, community, time, and place offer me for the meaningfulness I might make and the fact that it is my body located in this time and this place that allows certain things to coalesce in certain ways such that I end up having this particular experience, awareness, feeling, or understanding. How I come to that particular experience is not mere chance but is always connected to the general circumstances I share with others who are similarly situated. As a research procedure, phenomenology offers a set of methodological procedures through which we can investigate the very terms within which certain possibilities of human existence—over the exclusion of others—come to be actualized in the lived experience of persons. By examining the relationship between what is possible and what becomes actually present, phenomenology attempts to articulate the essential existential structures of what is present in the immediate lived experience of the person. At minimum, phenomenology offers a way of making more explicit than usual the experiential basis on which we might in fact be able to claim firmly that some kind of transformation in some aspect of the personal, social, or cultural world has occurred—and perhaps even that such transformation entails a throwing off of oppressive circumstances that otherwise would have remained.

Generally speaking, the application of phenomenological methodology involves stopping the natural flow of our conscious awareness, selecting an experience to focus on, suspending all of our presuppositions regarding that experience (i.e., we invoke the epoché), and describing it in as full detail as possible as if we are experiencing it for the first time in our description. After moving through the initial descriptive phase, phenomenological methodology requires an "imaginative variation" whereby we shift various aspects of the description around and re-see the experience and its many aspects in as many ways as possible. The purpose of the "imaginative variation" is to locate those features of the description that are essential to the experience itself. This is known as the reduction phase. The third general phase of phenomenological methodology is known as the interpretation phase. It is a continuation of the variations conducted in the second phase, but with an added effort to discover the preconscious terms in which the experience itself was possible. The interpretive phase involves a specification of existential meaning—that is, not just what I might say led me to think what I thought, feel what I felt, say what I said, or do what I did but the very terms in which this particular fact of experience became manifest among a field of many other possibilities. As we discover these essential existential structures of experience, we are also discovering the inherent sociality of the existential world. The essential existential structures we aim to discover are always already part of a social and cultural momentum in which every human consciousness is situated. Phenomenological research aims at the very juncture of human consciousness and the concrete social world in which it comes to be.

All this is very well and good, yet there is something inherently paradoxical about phenomenological methodology. First, it is very difficult to stop the natural flow of conscious awareness, even when we endeavor to do precisely that (perhaps those few persons who are highly accomplished in meditation are able to do so). It is equally difficult to actually suspend all of our presuppositions. No matter how faithful we are to the ideals of phenomenological methodology, there always remains a question regarding the extent to which we have put into the experience that which we claim to have discovered. Third, no matter how successful we might actually be in identifying the essential existential structure that has made a particular moment of existential meaningfulness possible, the structure changes upon our engaging it. We cannot escape the fact that time always runs ahead, around, and even behind us. There is a certain extent to which the application of any methodology is always out of step with the actuality of lived experience. The structuring of consciousness in lived-experience is always just that much beyond us as we attempt to specify the structures of consciousness that made a given moment of experience possible.

One might wonder how, in the face of such paradoxes, one could proceed with a phenomenological study. Here is how. These paradoxes of phenomenological methodology are, in fact, what make the methodology effective and appropriate for studying human being and becoming. The paradoxes themselves mean that the researcher her- or himself can never simply or finally arrive at a correct position or answer. The researcher is bound to the concreteness of lived experience whereby there is always an overflowing of meaning that can never be fully accounted for. By recognizing that there are limits in what can be accounted for, phenomenological research always remains open ended—that is, it never really ends. It is therefore bound to its own interrelation with others and the world. The proof or validity of phenomenological claims can be confirmed only by other *persons* equally engaged in the concreteness of lived experience and phenomenological reflection. However, the fact that phenomenological research never really ends creates another very important effect: The researcher is more strongly tied to the very existential terms and conditions through which the phenomenological study develops. As a result the researcher's movement through the methodological procedures will tend to be made more explicit. We recognize that we do indeed tend to discover only that which our own consciousness has put there for us to discover. So, we had better get busy accounting for precisely how it is that that thing itself became manifest. In this effort the researcher herself becomes more accountable to the relation between her own existential situation and the claims she comes to make. It is therefore the reader who finally must judge the adequacy of the epoché, imaginative variation, and specification of the essential existential structure. And this point is crucially important because we must all recognize that no matter how diligent and disciplined we are in our work, we are always handicapped by the partiality of our perspective and the omnipresent danger that we will delude ourselves by virtue of undetected personal, social, or cultural prejudices.

Herein lies the significance of phenomenological theory and methodology for the work of Chicanas, women of color, men of color, and other persons interested in social and cultural transformation. Chicanas, Chicanos, and other people of color who are racially and/or sexually marked recognize preconsciously that the social discriminations at work in the culture at large tend to put the legitimacy of our existence into question. We therefore face a choice at the level of the preconscious: either agree with the culture at large and risk coming to hate the difference in ourselves, our communities, and histories or disagree with the culture at large and begin what is a never-ending struggle to counter those dominant forces that mark us as questionable. From the perspective of the dominant culture, the former choice is the correct choice because it means that the person recognizes the need to "better himself," aspires to the norms and standards of the dominant culture, and will therefore be less able to critique the so-called naturalness or objectivity of those norms and standards. This choice perpetuates the taken-for-granted discriminations and keeps those discriminations safely away from any critique. The second choice, again from the perspective of the dominant culture, marks the person who critiques the dominant culture as pathological and unstable—which of course comes from and perpetuates the stereotypes already present in the dominant culture. Or, if not that response, then the person who critiques the discriminations carried in the dominant culture is asking for special favors and lowering the standards so that their inherent defect will not count against them. No matter what the person who is racially or sexually marked does, the dominant culture will tend to perpetuate—and even embrace—the racist and discriminatory logic that informs the initial identification of those persons whose legitimacy is in question. To the extent that phenomenology, as both a theoretical perspective and a research methodology, provides us with the means and tools to interrogate the very conditions in which those discriminations carried in the dominant culture are manifested and perpetuated in the everyday lived experience of persons is the extent to which we might be able to wedge open an otherwise tightly sealed closure that keeps racist and other discriminatory significations alive and circulating freely throughout the dominant culture.

The free and pervasive circulation of racism, sexism, and homophobia within the dominant culture means that the battle against these discriminations must be located at the level of the preconscious—a difficult battle to engage absent of a critique that illuminates these discriminations at the start. In other words, those who are racially and/or sexually marked within the dominant culture will, as much as anyone, tend to reproduce the tacitly accepted norms of that culture no matter the degree to which we ourselves are the objects of racism, sexism, and/or homophobia. Any phenomenological study that begins by accepting a naive notion of the possibility of a "pure" description will be less capable of breaking the hold of the tacitly accepted norms of the dominant culture. Nowhere is this more true than in the phenomenology of race, ethnicity, gender, class, and sexuality. The descriptive aspect of these phenomenological studies must start with critique. Descriptions of experience must be recognized as already being critical and interpretive. What keeps these phenomenological studies from becoming ideology or dogma is a continual putting into question the very terms and conditions by which this particular description became possible at this particular moment. This is the effort I take up in this text.

The work presented here sets itself in the middle of things ongoing. Theoretical arguments are laced with discussions of lived experience. Critical perspectives enable descriptions of experience, and descriptions of experience enable critical perspectives. Without the critical and experiential insights provided in the work of Chicanas, Chicanos, and other people of color, the descriptions here could never have come to be. Even still, much of the experience discussed here is my own. I present my experience not as a model, ideal, or exemplar of a "Chicana" but simply as the example to which I am necessarily tied. My effort is to make available to the reader the very terms and conditions through which I have come to say what I say here. For my Chicana audience especially, I hope that this work opens avenues for new critical and descriptive dialogues among us and with those who are interested in undoing the damages done by racist, sexist, classist, and homophobic cultures. For my non-Chicana audience, I hope that the work here reveals something of the huge contributions being made by Chicana studies. And I hope that those interested in transforming oppression and discrimination into opportunities for exertions of existential freedom and social liberation might find the phenomenological perspective offered here useful for further consideration.

ACKNOWLEDGMENTS

I am very fortunate to have had the support and encouragement of many people who have shown great care for me and this project over the past several years. If one measures one's fortune on the basis of the love and support that one receives from family and friends, then I am an incredibly fortunate person.

Patricia Huntington and Martin Matuštík, the editors of the series in which this book appears, have been tremendous supporters of the project. Patricia and Martin provided incredibly perceptive feedback on a very early draft of the manuscript. Their feedback was crucially important as I developed the work from its sketchy beginnings to its final version. It is not an overstatement to say that their ability to see the means and ways of the work that I was developing allowed me to move forward in ways I could not have otherwise. I am deeply grateful. Maureen MacGrogan, acquisitions editor at Rowman and Littlefield, was a big supporter of this project from early on. Her own comments on the manuscript were very helpful and remained a strongly guiding force as I worked through the final revision of it. All of the professionals at Rowman and Littlefield with whom I have worked have been of great assistance as I prepared the final manuscript. This work is much better for having been shepherded through the submission, review, and production process by such an outstanding group of professionals.

Berenice Carroll, director of the Women's Studies program at Purdue University, gets enormous credit for gently and consistently pushing and prodding me to put my work on Chicana feminism into a book. At a time when I found very little formal institutional support for my work on such a project, Berenice was adamant and persistent and showed unfailing belief in my work on this project. Without Berenice obviating the otherwise cool responses to the idea of this book, it might have never come to be. I cannot say enough about the degree to which Berenice's support has allowed me to believe in and pursue the activist work achieved in this text.

Cynthia Stohl, head of the Communication Department at Purdue University, deserves credit for her support during the last year of my work on this project.

There is a group of four people from whom I have had the benefit of detailed and sustained conversations over a period of years. Their reading and rereading of this work first in parts and then as a whole has been crucially important not only in the completion of this work but also in the spirit and commitment that drives it: Lisa Anderson, Linda Alcoff, Lewis Gordon, and Dorothy Leland. Dorothy deserves special credit for the idea of responding to our common experience of being whited with a public dialogue, which now appears as chapter six in this work. In addition, there are several people who have read versions of this work in part or whole. Their willingness to do so and their responses to me have been important to the development of it. I am grateful for their careful reading and responding: Bill McBride, Floyd Merrell, Pasty Schweikart, Floyd W. Hayes III, Dennis Mumby, Letticia Galindo, María Dolores Gonzales, Kristin Langellier, Cristina Gonzalez, and Thomas F. N. Puckett. Special acknowledgment must go to the students in my graduate seminars, "Phenomenologies of Race, Ethnicity, and Gender in the Study of Communication and Culture" and "Semiotic Phenomenology" for their eagerness to create a learning environment in which I learned so much. Thanks are also due to Terri Russ, who so willingly and supportively helped with some final details in the preparation of the manuscript.

I am very fortunate to have had teachers who are teachers in the fullest possible sense. I have benefited not only from their own learned backgrounds and skillful mentoring of young persons but even more from the rich examples of generosity, compassion, courageousness, and dignity that they have set for me: Richard Lanigan, Tom Pace, Alan Harris, and Tony Johnson. I have benefited from years of their guidance, care, and friendship. All of my successes, professional and personal, can be traced to key lessons that I have learned from each one of them.

There is another group of people to whom I owe a very special thank you: The Dojo. I have been incredibly fortunate over the past three years to be the sensei of Challenge Karate Club, Purdue University, where we train in traditional Shotokan karate. Over those three years, the members of Challenge Karate, and especially the Team members, have demonstrated an unfailing desire to dedicate themselves mentally and physically, day in and day out, to the ideals of traditional martial arts training. The big heart and big spirit that each one of them brings to their training, and therefore also to me, inspires me to never let them down by doing or becoming anything less than my absolute best.

Without the support of loved ones, family, and friends, I could have never generated or sustained the effort needed to take up the spirit directing my work on this project. Without these loved ones, I never would have been able to balance the demands of this work with the rootedness of knowing that in the end the only thing that matters is our relatedness to those we love: Lisa Anderson, whose loving partnership nurtures my heart; Angela and Luis Jaime, whose loving friendship sustains the best of what human beings can offer one another; and my sisters and brothers and nephews, with whom I have come to know and experience the greatest feelings of love and commitment: Jerri, David ("big D"), Mike and Cherrie, David ("little D") and Mathew, Teri, Jeff, and Justin. Finally, to my parents and grandparents, to whom I have always looked as I have sought to find my own way in life. Without each one of them—their care, sacrifices, and hopes for their children's futures—I could not have possibly found the inspiration to pursue the work and life presented here. It is out of respect and love for my parents, grandparents, and all the people mentioned here that I make my commitments not only for the work achieved here but also for the work of my whole life. I owe it to you all to give back so that others may benefit from all that you give me.

West Lafayette, Indiana

PERMISSIONS

Some of the material included here has been published previously. Chapter two is modified from "Speaking as a Chicana: Tracing Cultural Heritage and Betrayal" by Jacqueline M. Martinez in *Speaking Chicana: Voice, Power and Identity*, edited by D. Letticia Galindo and María Dolores Gonzales. Copyright © 1999 The Arizona Board of Regents. Reprinted by permission of the University of Arizona Press. An earlier version of chapter three, "Radical Ambiguities and the Chicana Lesbian: Body Topographies on Contested Lands," was published in *Spoils of War: Women, Cultures Revolutions*, edited by Tracy Sharply-Whiting and Renée T. White (1997). Chapter six, "Chicana y Chicana: A Dialogue on Race, Class, and Chicana Identity," is from *Readings in Cultural Contexts*, edited by Judith N. Martin, Thomas K. Nakayama, and Lisa A. Flores. Copyright © 1998 by Mayfield Publishing Company. Reprinted by permission of the publisher.

1

THE GENERATIVE NEXUS:
A CHICANA FEMINIST CROSSING

> It is by living my time that I am able to understand other times, by
> plunging into the present and the world, by taking on deliberately what
> I am fortuitously, by willing what I will and doing what I do, that I can
> go further.
>
> —Maurice Merleau-Ponty

The generative nexus from which this work emerges has many
aspects—subtle and obvious, direct and indirect, immediate and long
term, personal and professional. These aspects have led me collectively
and synergistically down what has often been an undetectable path leading to the production of this work. Taking as full an account as possible
of the synergism of these aspects is a necessary and recursive theme of
the project itself. The reasons why such a taking account is both necessary and recursive should become clear as the work progresses. For reasons that should also become clear as the work progresses, it is important
that I begin by taking account rather than by explaining why I am taking
account.

The fact that I hold a university position is the most obvious factor
in the generative nexus that is this work. My university position allows
me to spend my professional life immersed in teaching and engaging issues concerning the interconnections among communication, culture, history, and the social relations that make different moments of consciousness possible (semiotically, phenomenologically, and existentially). Like
all academic professionals, my specific academic training informs the what,
how, and why of my scholarly and teaching endeavors. There is no question that without my university position and scholarly training, this work
could not have come to exist. It is equally true, however, that these facts
of my professional life alone are far from accounting for the generative
nexus from which this text emerges. Like many academic professionals,
my formal scholarly and teaching endeavors bear an intimate, complex, and

sometimes conflicting relation with the whole of my encounters with self, others, and the unfolding of life and world. As important as they may be, these facts of my professional life are only one part of the generative nexus that spawns this work. Without the struggles of everyday life, of place and possibility, of history and remembering, this work simply could never have come to be. My professional scholarly training informs my theoretical orientation (semiotic and existential phenomenology) and constitutes one of two primary threads forming the generative nexus of this project. The second thread encompasses my own life experience and traverses the fabric of my growing up and adult life through a kind of temporal warp of the lived present, recollected past, and hoped-for future. The spinning and weaving of these two threads directs special attention to transformations in my own conscious experience and the specific critical awareness that spawned them. There are, unquestionably, very important scholarly and political reasons to take the lived experience of persons seriously. Yet, at various moments in my work on this project, the focus on my lived experience has felt incompatible with the more formal scholarly effort. The fact that I take my own lived experience as central to this work has at times seemed a misfit within the usual parameters of academic discourse, and I have wondered whether it would be possible to bring what appears to me as such different modes of expression together in a coherent and, it is hoped, relevant text.

The accomplishment of this bringing together that is this text itself constitutes a *border crossing*. But I must add quickly that the current popularity of border crossing as a theoretical construct gives me some concern for using it generally or without a specific, detailed, and situated discussion of what exactly this border is, how in fact it is crossed, and what is actually achieved or not. Only by detailing border crossing in this way may we lessen the risk of exploiting the wide variety of borders and people for whom crossing is anything but a popular concept of 1990s academic theorizing. I focus on this issue because it seems to me that in academic writing it is too easy to separate the theorizing about from the living through, to make a whole world out of one's introspective theorizations and thus evade asking the difficult but absolutely necessary question as to what degree the theorizing itself is or is not capable of speaking to communities and people situated socially, economically, politically, historically, and experientially differently than the theorist herself. For this reason (among others), I have relied a great deal on personal narrative and autobiography in the crafting of this work. Not only does such an approach make the work more accessible to a nonspecialized audience, but it also situates me very particularly as author and thus allows the reader to see not only the content of my thinking and theorizing but also the life experiences from which such thinking and theorizing emerges.[1] It is a small but important step in claiming a contribution to understanding and engaging a liberation effort. Talking about liberation is one thing; achieving it—particularly in writing for an academic audience—is a whole different matter indeed.

The question concerning the kind of difference academic writing can make in achieving actual liberation for even some of the countless number of communities and people in the United States who live as objects of economic, social, historical, and largely race-, class-, and/or sexuality-based oppression has halted my progress through this work from the very beginning. It has been difficult for me to believe heart and soul in my own academic writing as making that significant a difference. On the other hand, it has always been clear to me that in the classroom, in working with students, there is tremendous potential for pursuing radically liberating practices—a recognition that keeps me committed to the educational project as a learner. This fact, more than any other, has kept me in the academy and eases my otherwise troubling concerns about the limited audiences academic production serves. Thus, another important reason I have remained in the academy is the opportunity it offers me to take up a sustained study of people, issues, and communities to which I otherwise might not have access. Using both academic and nonacademic texts, I have taken up Chicana feminism as an area of study largely for my own personal and even selfish reasons. Through Chicana feminism I have been able to engage questions about myself and my familial heritage that I could not have taken up through any other kind of study. Yet the fact remains that I am an outsider to those communities that have been most heavily targeted by the racist-discriminatory forces of U.S. American culture and society. It has seemed to me that there is a certain risk in foregrounding my own experience to the exclusion of those who have suffered much more trying life circumstances than I have myself. And, as we know from the impressive work by David Goldberg (1993), *exclusions* are what racist culture is all about.[2] On the other hand, I have come to recognize how strategically important my own experience and understanding can be in fighting the forces of assimilation that lead many people with mixed ethnic and racial heritages (which means, in effect, everyone) to identify as primarily white and who thereby become part of a historical and social momentum that erases and denies the rich heritage of many people of color living in the United States. In this way, then, it becomes more possible to find alliance with a diversity of people of color who have widely ranging experiences of race, class, and sexuality but who nevertheless recognize a common enemy in the racist-assimilationist forces that direct much of the social, economic, and political discrimination in U.S. American culture.[3] It also becomes possible for me to experience the acute pleasure of discovering ways in which many aspects of my experience are typical with many Chicanas in this country and thus obviates that seemingly incessant need I feel to qualify my own identification as Chicana with "but I was raised in a white environment." In varying degrees and ways, *we all were.*

I take up Chicana feminism as an area of study that offers its own theory and methodology—that is, its own set of practices and self-understanding—that not only exemplifies successful movement against the racist-sexist-heterosexist-classist forces of the dominant U.S. American culture but that also is itself a unique contribution to the development of theory and methodology that serves the interests of those who are the objects of oppression. My own theoretical and methodological approach is grounded in semiotic and existential phenomenology. Despite the huge gap that often lies between the dense and abstract theorizing common in discussions of semiotics, existentialism, and phenomenology and the brash, fleshy, and "in your face" theorizing found in the expression of Chicanas and Chicana lesbians, I have found great resonance between Chicana feminism and semiotic and existential phenomenology. It is a resonance that emerges from the common concern with the lived body as the necessary site for struggle. This work is crafted from that resonance.

Taking up phenomenology to study race, ethnicity, class, sexuality, and power can be paradoxical in that the phenomenological effort requires a suspension of taken-for-granted categories such as race, ethnicity, and so on. Yet, if it is truly possible to suspend these categories, it can only be so by virtue of having traveled all the way through them—that is, by virtue of having interrogated and exorcised, if you will, every possible way in which racial, ethnic, economic, and sexual codes create contexts that preconsciously provide persons, groups, and cultures with ready-made significations about people and their circumstances that appear simply, naturally, to be true. In taking up this study, I do not want to privilege any of the labels used here as sufficient to define the work accomplished or the work accomplished as definitive of the abstract labels. I would rather privilege the *practice* engaged in this work. The practice engaged in this work entails a combination of Chicana feminism with semiotic and existential phenomenology. Not everyone engaging the practice of Chicana feminism will or need combine it with semiotic and existential phenomenology.[4] I do hope that others interested in Chicana feminism and issues of human freedom, transformations in consciousness, and racist culture might also look to semiotic and existential phenomenology—both as a discipline or field of study and even more as a way of interrogating the very condition of our social and historical realities. I also hope that those engaged in the study of semiotics, existentialism, and/or phenomenology will recognize and engage the important contributions made by Chicana feminism to our understanding of human and cultural existence. I most definitely do not want to leave the impression that the *theory* offered here is definitive of or conclusive for the study of race, ethnicity, class, and sexuality. That is because present work, such as that of Maurice Merleau-Ponty (1986) and the cinematic phenomenologist Vivian Sobchack (1992), aims "at the juncture of actual embodied praxis and its possibility." Thus, if the generalizations made within this work are "regarded as constituting a theory, [they] must be regarded paradoxically as a theory of the moment when there is no theory, when theory is both unthought and incomplete in its momentum as *praxis*" (Sobchack 1992, 214).[5] By its very nature, semiotic and existential phenomenology must be an open-ended inquiry that interrogates both its theoretical and its experiential conditions of possibility. The theory offered in this work is irrevocably linked to communication and praxis because my commitment to knowledge, understanding, and transformation is located in "the perceiving subject whose experience itself is never a final attainment, but an ongoing process of synthesis" (Lanigan 1991, 31). If liberating transformations in consciousness and the social world are to occur, it must be within the ongoing process of synthesis that is our personal and collective experience in the world.

Thus, it should be clear that in taking up Chicana feminism, I am *not* staking out a predetermined field of study with defined limits and exclusive rights to what happens within those limits. Although it is true that Chicana feminism has, over the past thirty years, become an identifiable field of study that can be said to have defined limits—and that it is legitimate, even important, to identify that field and those limits—that is not my purpose in the present work.[6] In other words, my commitment to Chicana feminism is not primarily as a defined field of study with its canonical texts and theoretical markers. My effort is avoid making Chicana feminism into an *object* of study static in my engagement with it. My orientation toward Chicana feminism—as I am certain it is for many Chicanas who take it up—has always been as a vehicle for discovery of self and world and never only as a field to know or a critical perspective to be applied. That does not mean, however, that I am not accountable to the history or field that is called Chicana feminism, that its critical insights are not important to take up and apply, or that I escape the burden of demonstrating why this communication, transformation, and praxis relationship I am advocating carries the particularities that we can recognize as Chicana feminism. My purpose is precisely to discover the possibilities of subjectivity and social transformation as lived and accounted for by the persons who come to take up Chicana feminism as a designator of self and therefore also a practice. Thus, in taking up this study I am bound to engaging the lived experience of real persons and the concrete, material, and historical realities in which we are situated. In this way, the work taken up here must be seen in terms of its (Chicana feminist) practice, as a

manner and style of thinking and being rather than simply (but impor-
tantly) a critical perspective, a recovery of history and perspective, or an
argument for public policies.[7] And I must point out that while I will be
concerned primarily with my own experiences and the experiences of those
who identify as Chicana feminists and/or Chicana lesbians, it is also true
that in many cases the experiences and insights discussed apply equally
well to other groups of U.S. women of color, women of color generally, and
any persons or groups who find themselves targets of socially generated
oppression. In fact, it is often the case that among groups who are objects
of oppression within a given society, a counterdiscourse of similar expression and strategy tends to emerge (Moraga and Anzaldúa 1983; Davis 1990;
Anzaldúa 1987, 1990; García 1989; hooks 1990; Mohanty et al. 1991;
Sandoval 1991; Darder 1995; High 1997).

COMMUNICATION AND RACIST-ASSIMILATIONIST FORCES

Ultimately, it is through communication that both the racist-
assimilationist forces and the alliances that form counterforces are created
or not, nurtured or destroyed. The question as to how one engages communicative practices that will tend toward either one of these possible ends
is a key question directing the current project. I approach communication
as embodied practice and recognize it as dynamically integral to any liberation effort—even one that uses academic writing as its primary form
of expression. My effort is to engage communication phenomenologically
as a reflection on and interrogation of the manners and styles of being of
those who struggle successfully against racial, sexual, class, and other oppression. It is by virtue of this interest that I come to identify the racist-
assimilationist forces of the dominant U.S. American culture as key in cri-
tiquing and usurping various oppressive structures and practices. In
addressing these points, I will be sketching a general orientation toward
communication and race, ethnicity, class, gender, and sexuality that informs
the whole of this work and that will be further developed and applied
throughout the text.

Communication is ubiquitous—it is everywhere, it surrounds us, it suffuses every moment of conscious life—and because of that we cannot
willfully escape it (except in the tragedy of suicide). While my speaking
and communicating may in fact be my own, particular to my body, gesture, and speech, it is also of the group, culture, time, and place—it is of
history, and it is anonymous. Communication is the means by which subjectivity (person) and sociality (world) are mutually constructed. Somewhere in this mutual construction, persons *experience* themselves, others,

and the world. In taking up communication, in whatever context and through whatever means, persons create experience—consciousness—and have the possibility of self-consciousness. Our very seeing, thinking, feeling, and acting always already partakes in the momentum of the social and discursive world. Our participation in this always already present momentum becomes habitual and constitutes a living habitus whereby persons unconsciously and preconsciously reconstitute and constitute the signifying systems that help give form to habitual practices in the first place—in a word, humans exist by way of praxis. Persons are bound habitually to others and the world by virtue of the inherently praxial nature of human communication.[8] Any given moment of human perception or expression constitutes a nexus point in a complex web of spatial, temporal, and semiotic boundedness between person (living body) and the social and discursive world. This boundedness is habituated in the life of the person, and therefore habit should be understood "*as a semiotic production*" that "*is both the result and the condition of the social production of meaning*" (De Lauretis 1984, 179 [emphasis in the original]). Communication is a fact of human praxis that speaks both to the formation of human subjectivity and to the material and concrete world through which all subjectivity comes to existence in expression and perception.

The formation of subjectivity, while not disconnected from the uniqueness and particularity of each person, is nonetheless inextricably and endlessly in communication with the anonymity of history and the parameters of the social and discursive worlds through and around which every particular human being comes to experience subjectivity intersubjectively (Merleau-Ponty 1986; Lanigan 1988).[9] Transformations of consciousness and the social world are therefore possible because both consciousness and the parameters of discourse are inextricably located *in communication* between person and history. To see these parameters—*to see oneself seeing what one sees by virtue of them*—is to have the capacity to change them as they are created and lived in experience. That fact, however, does not make the deliberate effort to transform consciousness or the social world direct, easy, or a sure outcome in any stretch of the imagination—such an effort can be (often is) hopelessly naive. It is the case, for example, that liberal-modernist struggles against racism presuppose the taken-for-granted "nature" of race, thus reproducing the conditions through which we recognize racial difference, in turn perpetuating racist exclusions within the very struggle itself (Goldberg 1993, 33).[10]

By virtue of our inextricable *being-in-communication-with*, persons and history are capable of habits of self-deception, denial, willful and self-serving ignorance, and arrogant self-justification.[11] When history (anonymously) denies or arrogantly justifies the fact of social and discursive discrimination based on the exclusion of racialized persons as meeting the standard for human being (or, at best, recognized as being inferior humans), we have an all-encompassing cultural disposition (*Zeitgeist*) that perpetuates the features necessary for a racist culture. Within such a racist culture, that which constitutes race, racism, and the racialization of particular persons or groups is *not* singular or static. This is the thesis developed by Goldberg (1993), who argues that our very notion of race responds to varying transformations in the social and discursive world and thus continually and perniciously re-creates itself as an exclusion. We recognize in Goldberg's thesis the Foucauldian (1972a) focus on discovering the rules of transformation governing discourse that lead to the formation of objects and thus also subjects within discourse. Goldberg's task, then, is to "account for the emergence, transformation, and extension, in a word, the (continuing re-) invention of racist culture, and for the varying kinds of discursive expression that it prompts and supports" (1993, 8). In engaging precisely this effort, Goldberg observes that racialized discourse and racist expression cannot be explained "solely in socioeconomic, political, or sociological terms" because such accounts ignore "the *persuasiveness* of racist expression, its compelling character for subjects" (1993, 57 [emphasis added]). Indeed, one must account for the fact that persons who are racialized in and who employ racialized discourse hold "conscious belief and conviction, or [a] rational willingness" to go along with such racializations. Given this fact, "the question of human agency and the formation of subjectivity must be addressed." Being-in-communication-with, as an inextricable fact of human existence, places both persons and the parameters of discourse in communication and allows us access to the processes through which racialized discourses—and the varying signifying contents they hold—carry enough persuasive force to become habitual (though not necessarily self-consciously apparent) in the consciousness of persons, groups, and cultures.

The fact that we inhabit a living body that is located in time and space makes it possible that in our own conscious experience we have varying degrees of reflective and reflexive access to the parameters of the social and discursive world that we take up habitually and through which we become our subjectivity intersubjectively. This is possible by virtue of *intentionality*: the fact that human consciousness always has a content—consciousness is always consciousness of something. Similarly, to experience is always to have an experience of something (Ihde 1986, 42). In this way, consciousness and experience are irreducibly *directional*—that is, both consciousness and experience are always in movement toward. The inherent and ceaseless motility of consciousness and experience is thus an essential aspect of intentionality. Every moment of human perception is made possible by virtue of intentionality. In this way, "perception is always already the *expression* of intentionality in the world" (Sobchack 1992, 69–70). The moment I perceive something, it is because I have already been disposed to see that which I perceive. Thus, my *perception is always already an expression.* Intentionality is "the condition of possibility for all experience to be shaped in a certain way. . . . Intentionality is the directional shape of experience" (Ihde 1986, 41). This is so because intentionality is irreducibly correlational in that every content of consciousness and experience is both *noematic* (it has a *that* which one is conscious of or a *that* which is experienced) and *noetic* (it has a *mode* of being conscious of, or a *mode* of experiencing). The fact that consciousness is always directed and correlational makes the fact of intentionality transcendental and static in the ironic sense that consciousness never stops moving, always has an orientation or a directedness toward, and is anchored in the lived body. The form (mode) and content (what) of that directedness, however, is never static or transcendental. Rather, the contents of consciousness and experience are always *contingent, situated,* and *existential.*[12] Because we exist in and through our lived body, "intentionality is *expressed* by the body-subject living in the world; it becomes manifest, *signified . . .* the lived body is the signifier of intentionality, but it is so only in its action as an existence that intends, only in its *activity of signifying*" (Sobchack 1992, 65).[13] As the "agency and agent of intentionality, the lived-body can be considered the *sign-vehicle* of intentionality" (Sobchack 1992, 73–74).

Intentionality, as irreducibly correlational, is inextricably woven within our habitual ways of being in the world. In this sense, habitual should be understood as a "tendency toward action," a "readiness" or "disposition toward action" (Peirce, *Collected Papers,* vols. 1–8, 1931–1958, cited in de Lauretis 1984, 178). Thus, we understand intentionality as a directional flow through (that helps re-create and create) a complex web of spatial, temporal, and semiotic boundedness between person (living body) and the social and discursive world such that any moment of human perception or expression constitutes a nexus point in this semiotic boundedness. It therefore becomes possible to interrogate the noetic-noematic correlate of that directedness and thereby discover that which was present but invisible (the noematic made possible by virtue of the noetic; the interpretant produced in the use of the sign) in the constitution of our habit or tendency-toward in the first place. It also creates the possibility of changing that habit. Teresa de Lauretis's (1984) explanation of this dynamic is worthy of lengthy quotation:

> When Peirce speaks of habit as the result of a process involving emotion, muscular and mental exertion, and some kind of conceptual representation . . . he is thinking of individual persons as the subjects of such processes. If the modification of consciousness, the habit or habit change,

is indeed the meaning effect, the "real and living" conclusion of each single process of semiosis, then where "the game of semiosis" ends, time and time again, is not exactly in "concrete action," as Eco sees it, but in a disposition, a readiness (for action), a set of expectations. Moreover, if the chain of meaning comes to a halt, however temporarily, it is by anchoring itself to somebody, some body, an individual subject. As we use or receive signs, we produce interpretants. Their significate effects must pass through each of us, each body and each consciousness, before they may produce an effect or an action upon the world. *The individual's habit as a semiotic production is both the result and the condition of the social production of meaning.* (178–179)

Thus, we understand that the living body is essentially linked both in the intentional structure of consciousness and in the semiotics of habit formation and change. The identification of habits—as a semiotics of the living body as it expresses (signifies) intentionality—is the proper terrain from which change in the social production of meaning may be pursued.

By virtue of our habituated ways of being-in-the-world, the lived body is bound semiotically to the social and discursive world in which it is situated. Identifying these habits of consciousness and experience is possible because intentionality—the very modality through which habits of being are taken up and re-created is also always inherently *diacritical.* That is, the moment of perception already marks a choice, is an assigned value, and carries significance from the social and discursive world within which we come to perception. "Significance and signification," as Sobchack puts it, "co-emerge with the directional movements of the finite lived-body— for as the lived-body intends *toward* one object of consciousness, it necessarily turns *away* from another. Thus, a *choice* is made, a *value* ascribed and inscribed. Such choices occur even when it is not explicitly willed and, indeed, remains latent as the background against which deliberate choices stand out as willed" (1992, 65). One does not have to consciously choose to be racist, but by virtue of the habits informing the movement of intentionality across its noetic-noematic correlation, the signs of race already carry significations within the conscious experience of persons. Perception is always already a judgment. The fact that racial categories are fundamental to our immediate perception of self and others and that the dominant culture spends so much effort asserting that its communities are not racist suggests that race is an important (even essential) aspect of the "already interested and engaged existence" that is our current human situation (Sobchack 1992, 71). It also suggests more than a little bit of cultural denial at work in the assertion that race is not a factor of judgment or experience.

If we understand that habits of consciousness and experience are a function of the lived body's semiotic boundedness to the social and discursive world, then it follows that the lived body is also connected to a history—not merely a history of that body's conception, birth, and growth but also of that body as a cultural body that carries the flow and pressures from previous generations forward as well as the expectations of a likely future backward. The cultural body, like the lived body of the person, embodies the terms of its very existence. The cultural body is inextricably in-communication-with its own notion of itself and is, like the lived body of the person, capable of self-deception, denial, and arrogant self-justification. When the sixteenth-century European imperialists "discovered" the "new world," they created for themselves an Other against which the possibilities for their own sense of Self were posed (Goldberg 1993). Some have even gone so far as to suggest that "it is in fact the conquest of American that heralds and establishes our present identity" (Todorov 1992, 5). Todorov marks Columbus's voyage as the transition from medieval to the modern time, Columbus himself being a character with a medieval commitment to God and Christianity and a modern commitment to naming and categorizing nature. The "discovery" of America, Todorov argues, was unique in the context of European imperialism. Whereas European encounters with Asia and Africa were encounters with the already known, the encounter with the native peoples of the western hemisphere had no such preknowing. This fact, Todorov argues, made the "new world" unique in the way in which the Self could be counterposed to the Other. It is a counterposing that is essentially racial and racist. As Goldberg (1993) puts it, "Since 1500, then, race has been the subject of intense political and epistemological contestation and through which it has variously assumed the symbolic power to colonize the prevailing terms of social interpretation, habit, and expression—to dominate, without quite silencing social discourses" (81). Race and racial identification, it can thus be argued, constitutes an omnipresent force in the living cultural body as it moves across generations over hundreds of years. Todorov's study of the "conquest of America" focuses on the perceptions of the Spanish explorers, conquerors, and clergymen in their encounters with the native people. In their efforts to understand the native people, the Spaniards enacted an "understanding that kills" and began what has become the most devastating and long lasting genocide of human history. These facts are telling when one considers the inherent reversibility of perception and expression. The imperialists' perception is always already an expression of an arrogantly assumed superiority of their own culture and the self-justifying and ceaseless effort to dominate, desecrate, and destroy the Other (themselves). The fact that perception is always already an expression, a choice, a value that makes the perception what it is confirms that the fact of genocide is at root possible because of the idea of a superior Self counterposed to an inferior and primitive Other carried in the European imagination: "American Indians and inhabitants of Africa were imagined in European representations considerably before their exploitation as slaves took place. Indeed, these images and the discursive rationalizations attendant with them enabled the conceivability of Euro-enslavement of colonial inhabitants" (Goldberg 1993, 53). This is a sign of a sick culture.

As long as history operates from, yet denies, a sense of racial difference and therefore (white, European) "superiority," it will be possible for culture, groups, and persons from a wide variety of racial and ethnic heritages to identify with white, European superiority and thus guarantee the perpetuation of a cultural sickness whereby there must always be some (dark-skinned primitive others) who are known and believed to be inferior humans, if they are even recognized as human at all. The internalization of this fundamental dynamic of history and culture will always work most insidiously against those who are marked by the signs of skin color (black), speech (nonnative or nonstandard English), and community (barrio, agricultural field, sweatshop, or ghetto) and are thus perceived as inferior, less than, or unable within the terms of the dominant culture. It simultaneously works in favor of those who by virtue of the same signs are unmarked and considered simply normal. It is no surprise, then, that efforts to direct one's conscious awareness toward one's own conscious experience of race, ethnicity, culture, and so on comes most predominantly from those who are marked as different and therefore also the targets of oppression within the dominant culture. It is by virtue of this effort that persons who are the objects of social and cultural oppression seek to undo the dehumanizing internalizations promoted by the dominant society and its cultural body's history.

The identification of habits as they exist at the level of the living body expressing intentionality allows the possibility of changing those habits of the level of noetic-noematic correlation that is intentionality. This is a particularly important effort given the extent to which contemporary U.S. American culture takes for granted race, gender, class, and sexuality as real and natural designators of persons. We may reduce the persons we come in contact with to those designators to varying degrees, but to the degree that the designators remain legitimate as designators is the degree to which the culture retains its enabling disposition toward racism, sexism, homophobia, and so on. In other words, many persons living with such a culture will have widely varying notions of what race is—that is, noematically there will be many differing ideas of what race represents, how important it is, and what kind of basis it does or does not establish for judgments of self and others. Some people will invoke racialized knowledge more strongly than others, and those who do so "mildly" are able to say, "I am not racist." Yet both the person who invokes racialized knowledge "mildly" and the one who invokes it virulently (the self-acknowledged racist) rely on a cultural disposition that takes for granted the accuracy of racial distinction. Both persons rely on a certain content of racialized knowledge. Regardless of the existence of "mildly" invoked racializations, such racializations—as much as the virulently racist racializations—establish all the necessary conditions for the perpetuation of a racist culture within which virulently racist persons will continue to be produced. By interrogating the social production of meaning as it passes through each living body in exact moments of noetic apprehension, we have the capacity, at least at a local level, to change the very terms by which race, gender, class, or sexuality come to have the meanings they do. It is a change that must occur at the reflexive (not reflective) and habituated level of consciousness coming to take up that which it takes up in the very living body of persons. Such a strategy does not result in the elimination of racial categories but rather alters their meaning-generating capacity at the noetic level.

Recognizing the way in which culture, groups, and persons are racist, sexist, homophobic, intellectualist, classist, and so on and arguing for change in the ways we preconsciously understand ourselves as women who are also racially marked and often economically poor is one part Chicana feminism's effort to change the very terms in which it is possible to conceive of oneself, others, and the world. This is particularly true with the emergence of contemporary Chicana lesbian work (Moraga and Anzaldúa 1983; Anzaldúa 1987, 1990). This body of work—most decidedly *not* written for academic consumption of the traditional sort—challenges readers and teachers of the work to rethink the very ways in which we preconsciously take up ideas of race, ethnicity, sexuality, and the assumed superiority of normalcy: a white middle-class heterosexual existence. I do not need the language of intentionality and its noetic-noematic correlation to understand as I read Moraga and Anzaldúa (1983) that I am challenged to change my very disposition toward myself, my history, and my world.

I have a passionate identification with Chicana feminism. It is a passionate identification discovered by virtue of a lived-body recognition that began preconsciously in the most subtle and gradual of ways. It is an identification that has grown and developed as I have consciously taken up the dynamic interrelations among my lived social-familial history, my day-to-day struggles of place and possibility, and my formal scholarly research and writing. I am a Chicana lesbian who has spent the majority of her professional academic career engaging issues precisely about the presence of Chicanos and Chicanas in the United States, the influences of culture and society that result in the particular orientation I was raised to have toward my Mexican American ancestry, and the effects of being the daughter of a father who "made it" in mainstream U.S. American society. It has been only by virtue of my recognition of a deep-seated correlation between my own barely conscious (noetic) access to my lived experiences of race and ethnicity (noema) that I have been able to engage a formal scholarly effort to consider how notions of race, ethnicity, gender, sexuality, and culture combine to create very specific possibilities for human and social becoming. My life experiences have provided essential points of entrée into my larger concern with communication, culture, and human becoming. In this way, the "facts" of my life that I offer throughout this work are taken as *signs* of a certain time and place that, when taken out of their normally non-reflected-on state, allow for a certain kind of critical investigation to go forward. It is important to emphasize again, however, that these "facts" themselves are *not* the subject matter for investigation or the circumstances that constitute explanations.[14] Rather, because this investigation takes seriously the irreducible subjectivity that is carried in intentionality and thus can never be removed from any human expression, be it artistic, scientific, political, intellectual, or whatever, I am bound to engaging that subjective presence and its intentionality explicitly. Taking that subjective presence in human expression seriously means that the analytic and critical rigor of the work itself lies in an interrogation at the reflexive level and thus also as the very methodology guiding the movement and development of it. Again, it is important to emphasize that what we are interrogating is not simply introspective self-reflection, where a consciousness reflects on what one is conscious of, but a self-reflexivity where the immediate linkages that allow for particular contents of consciousness to manifest in the first place are discovered. In semiotic terms, I am interested in Peirce's *interpretant* as a hidden but enabling representation that makes possible the more commonly knowable sign and its meaning. The interpretant does not function like a stabilizing or undergirding code that once revealed tells us "exactly what really is." Rather, interrogating the interpretant as it makes meaningfulness manifest in human experience (similar to interrogating intentionality) locates us in a realm of *unlimited semiosis* where every sign requires an interpretant, which is itself a sign requiring an interpretant, and so on ad infinitum.

If we take seriously the fact of unlimited semiosis as an essential fact of human existence, then our most basic notions of time, the significance of time's passage, and its apparent linear and sequential character must be called into question. That is to say, by taking seriously the ongoing action of signs and their open-ended capacity for signification, we recognize the impossibility of stopping, capturing, or making bare any one moment of experience. That is because what I experience in one moment is different from the sense I make of that experience in the next moment. There is a certain order of experience that will always be different from the order of analysis. No matter how faithfully I track back through time to an exact experience, that tracking will always be of a different temporal order than the experiencing itself. Yet even this understates the case of unlimited semiosis and the temporality of human existence. Although we can say simply that the present will always affect our recounting of the past, it is also true that our anticipated future affects what we come to experience of the present and the past. That is not to say, however, that an anticipated future so overrides the present and our recollections of the past that the latter two are mere phantoms of subjective creation. There is a facticity to our concrete experience in a specific time and place, and the concreteness of time and place will always function interrelatedly with how we come to make any sense of any moment in time. The experience itself is both in the concreteness of time and place and in the spiraling action of semiosis that entails an anticipated future, recollected past, and experienced present.

Consider the very common example of a middle-class Latina or black woman traveling on business and staying at an upscale hotel where a white woman mistakes her for a maid. Prior to recognizing that she has been mistaken for a maid, she assumed that the white woman approaching her was going to say any number of things that two strangers staying at the same hotel might say to each other. On recognizing, however, that the white woman assumes her to be a maid, she is taken aback and may respond in any number of ways. The white woman's ability to mistake the woman of color for a maid was made possible by an enabling interpretant that she used preconsciously to form the idea that the woman of color was a maid. The appearance of the woman of color in her field of vision did not *cause* her to see the woman of color as a maid. What enabled that vision was an interpretant that mediated the objective signs (skin color, clothing, context, and so on), which then led to the meaning she constructed: That woman is a maid. It seems plausible to suggest that any woman of color is at risk for being mistaken as a maid in any upscale hotel in the United States—the interpretants generated and regenerated around the sign of race-gender are so common and taken for granted that they create deeply seeded dispositions or habits. Let us say that the white woman explains her mistake by saying that the woman of color was dressed in clothes that could be taken for "maidlike." Such an explanation evades the most obvious interpretant mediating between woman and maid: the fact that the woman was not white. The white woman might explain away her mistake as a simple (mild) one, not a sign of any racist intent, and thus not take any special notice of what her error might reveal about her very disposition toward people who fit different racial designations. Should the white woman take this strategy, she will simply re-create the interpretants that allowed that mistake (and no doubt others like it) to occur in the first place. Although the white woman is forced to correct her error in this particular instance, nothing has changed at the level of the general (noetic) disposition that allowed her to make the mistake in the first place. If, however, the white woman were to make conscious to herself the way in which the racial category that she took for granted *allowed* her to make the error she did, she might change her very perception (already an expression) and make different judgments in future encounters but also, and perhaps more important, resignify racialized perceptions and judgments she has made in the past. In this case, each moment of resignification creates new interpretants that do not simply carry forward the commonly assumed and stereotyped content of racialized knowledge. It is in this sense, then, that we say that once we have entered into the realm of unlimited semiosis, our notion of how temporality functions changes—we can no longer take for granted a linearity of temporality where one moment moves into a future moment as if experience is the building up of bricks to construct a wall. Tracing through racial significations cannot be limited to an assumed sequence of past to present or even of present to past. Rather, our understanding of the past and hopes for the future must be interrogated as present in each moment of perception and expression. From each moment in the present, our understanding of the past and hopes for the future may be re-created so as to maintain the same habits or dispositions or so as to change those habits or dispositions. Ironically, we need the passage of time in its apparently linear progression to "look back" and see maintenance or change. It is just that on seeing *that*—something else has emerged allowing us to see it *as that*. That something else is the interpretant, which may itself help maintain or change habit or disposition and so on ad infinitum.

For people who are the object of racialized knowledge, then, the question whether they are or are not actually what the stereotype would have them to be gives way to the question as to how it is that others in general will continue to see them in that way. It makes no difference that the Latina or black woman who is mistaken for a maid is actually a successful businessperson—she will always be at a certain risk for being seen as a maid. This dynamic of culturally generated perception also creates circumstances where middle-class Latinos and blacks are considered "not really" Latino or black because they do not live in the ghetto or barrio and/or do not speak with the ghetto or barrio dialect. Yet, in recognizing the dynamic way in which racialized perception and knowledge continues to create itself in an unlimited semiosis, we see that the question of authentic ethnic or racial origin must give way to the question of which linkages or associations have allowed what to be carried forward. For racially and ethnically marked others, the desire to identify some mythical time before oppression to which we seek to return is offset by the recognition that we are bound to a present in which certain possibilities within the living through of a critically engaged consciousness might have the capacity to usurp oppressions otherwise reproducing themselves in the very habits and actions of people individually and collectively. It is the mediating function of interpretants that enable the naturalness of the representation to be re-created and sustained throughout a culture and its history. It is in this way that we understand notions of race, gender, sexuality, or class as *technologies* that allow for the ongoing normative naturalization of them (Foucault 1972a; De Lauretis 1987; Goldberg 1993).

To restate the case, notions of racial or ethnic heritage are representations (enabled by interpretants) that also become self-representations (thus creating new interpretants that maintain or change the content of the representations). I come into a world of ready-made ethnic and racial representations that do or do not become self-representations based on notions of my own and others' nature—I either am or am not black; Spanish either is or is not my first or predominant language; I can either take the security of my housing, food, and clothing situation for granted or I cannot; and so on. The moment I recognize myself (preconsciously) as on one side or another of those representations, they become self-representations. But in making them self-representations, they do not simply replicate the given representations themselves. Rather, the representations themselves become producers of representations in those very moments in which I preconsciously take them up. This is an especially salient point when one considers the massive flow of racial and ethnic representations that suffuse virtually every kind of mass communication, the awesome materiality of discourse (to borrow a phrase from Foucault), and the way in which the person, situated as an active nexus point within this complex of communication and temporality, habitually takes up these ready-made representations and makes of them self-representations. It is precisely this dynamic of sociality or sociogeny that leads Fanon (1967) to say, "There is one destiny for the Black man, and it is white" (10). Theoretically and methodologically speaking, this work is an effort to critically, analytically, and reflexively examine the habits of a certain consciousness (my own); the technologies of race, gender, sexuality, and class through which it is (I am) produced and producing; and its (my) relationship to a particular time and place in the ongoing movement of history.

To the extent that the dominant culture is racist, sexist, and homophobic, all persons living and communicating within that culture will tend to re-create racism, sexism, and homophobia even as it diminishes one's own sense of self and community.[15] Yet not all persons will re-create the general sensibilities of the dominant culture in exactly the same way. Operating with a common racist logic, some will make it explicit by using a racial slur or advocating the superiority of the "white race," while others may make a judgment based on a racial stereotype and deny the stereotype as the source of judgment.[16] Some will operate under the belief that they are treated equally, like all other people, until the day comes that they realize that they have always been marked and have never been just like everyone else. If, by virtue of such a realization, one directs one's own conscious awareness toward their own conscious experience, we have a "practice of self-consciousness" where it is possible to exert a counterforce against the prevailing sensibilities of culture. In the context of feminist theory and practice, this "practice of self-consciousness" has directed itself toward "one's personal condition as a woman in terms social and political, and the constant revision, reevaluation, and reconceptualization of that condition in relation to other women's understanding" (De Lauretis 1987, 20). Similarly with race and ethnicity: To the extent that one sees through the racist norms of culture as they are taken up in the communicative practices of oneself and other persons, one is capable of revisioning, reevaluating, and reconceptualizing those norms as they function within their own conscious experience. If one is both a woman (a lesbian, let's say) and a member of a racially marked category (a Chicana, let's say), then the possibility of revisioning, reevaluating, and reconceptualizing cuts across both general categories and works against the modernist tendency to *arrive* at a set of just cultural norms. In other words, if by virtue of being of color the lesbian recognizes racism within white communities, her being a lesbian might also alert her to homophobia within her communities of color. Thus, there is no single "ism" to fight, no single community toward which to turn, and no single perspective on history that can allow her to decide simply what is just (Moraga 1983). Continuing with this line of thinking, it follows that those who occupy positions within culture that are the most multiply marked or marginalized would be more capable than others to expose the racist, sexist, and other unjust aspects of the dominant culture.[17] Yet not all persons who are marginalized—singly, doubly, or multiply—within the dominant culture come to critique it. There is an aspect of indeterminability about the fact of human situatedness in time, space, and culture and the particular consciousness of that situatedness that any given person may have. What makes the difference between those who see through the oppressive practices of a given social place and time and those who come to internalize the logics that inform those practices? This is a key question that occupies the whole of the current project. But for a different set of circumstances, I might very well have never come to any of the conscious reflections that have made this work possible.

If we are to pose an explicit answer to this question, it can come only by way of a certain kind of praxis, a *mestizaje* praxis that informs the whole of this work and leads me particularly to place myself, my lived experiences and personal feelings, squarely within it. For a *mestizaje* praxis to be a *mestizaje* practice, it must have some degree of self-consciousnesses for the person engaging it as a *mestizaje* praxis. It need not necessarily be named as such, but there must be some awareness of the conflicting codes (borderlands) across which one struggles creatively and constructively— that is, struggles by creating new interpretants and building bridges across long separated spaces (lands). As I shift below to a more personal consideration of the facts of my own time and place, consciousness, and self-consciousness, I will be engaging a manner and style of being through which I hope a praxis of deassimilation may come forth. The shift to a more personal style of discourse is important because it is ultimately in my own contact with the world through my lived body that I can gain reflexive access to the very movement of intentionality and the signifying relations that make experiences of consciousness possible in my own life (although that does not mean that I will necessarily be successful in this effort or that I am not also capable of self-delusion). Equally important, the shift to the fact of my own time and place brings this work back to its being-in-communication-with, back to the very conditions by which it was possible in the first place—it makes the work more (though not necessarily adequately) accountable to the fact of a lived body, a person's experience, the cultural body from which those experiences are possible and the very process through which conscious experience becomes experiences of consciousness.

THE VALLEY

In order to adequately flesh through the generative nexus from which this text emerges, it is necessary to ask the question as to how it is that someone like me comes to take up the question of Chicano and Chicana identity in the first place. After all, ever since the first landings of Spaniards on the North American continent, there have been many people with Spanish surnames inherited through every generation on this land. Why should having the surname Martinez, when attached to all the signs of success in middle-class achievement in U.S. mainstream culture, signify to self and others anything other than the success of the "melting pot"? Why should having such a name attached with such signs provoke any kind of reflection on the origin and meaning of it? Spanish surnames blanket the landscape of this country and especially in the West and Southwest. I grew up in the San Fernando Valley, which lies about thirty-five miles northwest of downtown Los Angeles ("city of the angels").[18] The Valley itself is full of names oddly juxtaposed. I grew up in the northwest part of the Valley, in the postal districts known as Northridge and Chatsworth. But there were boulevards named Sepulveda and Balboa. The Spanish-Mexican and Anglo-European names lived side by side without any cause for notice in my growing-up world. Granada Hills was nearby, and like the more Anglo-Saxon named "Woodland Hills," the "Hills" designator seemed to obviate any Spanish-Mexican association that might have been attached to "Granada." But the postal district of "San Fernando," located in the northeast part of the Valley, also happened to be a place generally identifiable as the barrio, "low-rider" territory where the predominantly Mexican American community was economically poor, youth were in gangs, kids were streetwise, and thus the social signs of criminality dominated. There was also the postal district of Reseda, right next to Northridge, which we came to call "little Mexico," where illegal aliens (we assumed) lived crowded into one-bedroom apartments and stood on the street corners wearing dirty T-shirts and polyester pants with broken zippers. My family lived in a cozy six-bedroom ranch-style home with a three-car garage, swimming pool, large country kitchen, formal dining room, and two fireplaces.

Today I know that Ginés de Sepúlveda, the Spanish scholar and philosopher who lived in the mid-sixteenth century, argued that the native peoples of the "new world" were "as inferior to the Spaniards as children are to adults and women to men." Sepúlveda argued that "there is as great a difference between them [and Spaniards] as there is between savagery and forbearance, between violence and moderation" and used the comparison "as between monkeys and men" (quoted in Todorov 1992, 153; see also Las Casas 1992; Leon-Portilla 1992). As a child who knew that Sepulveda Boulevard was "that way" and that it could take me "over there," this name, like nearly all the others, signified primarily a line in space that bore a relation to the other lines by which I could navigate the world around me, the street layout of the Valley being primarily gridlike. Yet the significance of this street name, like so many other designators of geography, far exceeds the effect of simply fixing a line or place in space. How are we to assess the significance of names and place inherited from a time so long ago? What kind of critical analysis of "Sepulveda Boulevard" is warranted when Sepúlveda, the person who lived in the sixteenth century, articulated some of the earliest and most evil words of racist exclusion, and helped pave the way for a justification of the massive genocide that was to take place? What kind of critical connection can be drawn between a young man named Octavio Martinez (my father) settling with his family in the San Fernando Valley in the mid-twentieth century and the history of racism and racist exclusions that suffuses generations that preceded him? How are we to critique the diachronicity of name and attitudes from centuries back and the synchronicity of a person simply trying to "make it" in a given moment of history?

"Sepulveda Boulevard" is not so named by happenstance; it comes *derived* from a "continuous movement of words from their source or origin" that functions not as a "single stable bond that links one root to one representation" but rather with a slippage in those very links carried in the name itself (Foucault 1970, 115). In this continuous diachronic movement of slipping representation also comes a content, a *proposition*. Derivation carries a proposition because "without it all designation would remain folded in on itself and could never acquire the generality that alone can authorize a predicating link" (Foucault 1970, 115). The Spanish-Mexican names that blanket the western and southwestern United States are a direct sign of the cultural imperialism perpetuated on it. In this way derivation functions spatially—the names of the colonialist culture define the very space itself. The fact that over time the boulevard named Sepulveda gradually loses all direct signification with the sixteenth-century racist scholar and becomes instead simply a line in space that is "that way" and can take me "over there" reveals how proposition functions as a linear phenomenon. Bit by bit and sequentially, the names, which when first applied signified immediately the person or place from which it was derived, recede until eventually there is no discernable link with the source from which the name was derived. The propositional content of those signs changes. The accompanying *articulative* capacities of language at any one moment in time—that is, what is possible to speak with a language—is connected directly to the derivations achieved in space and the propositions carried across time. As Foucault (1970) puts it, this relation of derivation and articulation defines language's "historical posture and its power of discrimination" (116). Thus, it is overly simple—but not completely incorrect—to say that by living in an assimilationist-racist culture where names of the colonialist oppressors are blanketed across the geography, we have all lived under the discriminations advocated by Sepúlveda and continued by those who followed him. It is entirely incorrect, however, to say that the fact that the boulevard is named "Sepulveda" is insignificant. As I was growing up from the mid-1960s to the mid-1980s in the Valley, I had every reason to naively follow along with the voiceless names that suffused the discursive world of that time and place.

The American Dream of upward social mobility provides hope that if you are born poor you do not have to remain poor, that your children might be better off than you were. Hope is an important thing. If you believe in the Dream, believe in yourself, manage to get education, and have a good bit of luck, you may indeed find yourself advancing up in the socioeconomic scale of U.S. American society. Yet this is just one scenario of how the American Dream works. There is a sinister side as well. The mere existence of the Dream legitimates that there will always be those who have not achieved it; it authorizes the notion that those who have not made it up the socioeconomic scale deserve to be at the bottom. And it removes social accountability to even the most horrifically poor, destitute, and socially isolated communities within society. The pervasiveness of the

American Dream in the psyche of U.S. American culture creates a whole series of double binds for those living in poverty-stricken environments, with poor education being surrounded by the most virulent racist stereotyping and the inevitably self-deflating encounters with mainstream U.S. American culture. In this way, the American Dream authorizes the existence of incapacitated communities where life is defined by fighting daily battles for basic survival. In such an environment, the simple but profound achievement of a person's sense of human dignity becomes a crucial measure of success, albeit a success unrecognized within the narrow terms of the American Dream. I am the daughter of a man who, thanks to his parents' own sense of human dignity, made it out of poverty's often deadening grip on self-respect and who was then fortunate enough to make it out of the economic conditions that keep people locked into chronically impoverished and otherwise constrained communities.

My father's determination to succeed directed him into the belly of an Anglo world. He became fully integrated into the Anglo world because that was where the possibilities for success lay. Although fully bilingual as a child, my father's movement into the Anglo world closed the space for his Mexican-mestizo cultural difference to be explicitly embraced or carried to his children. This aspect of my family heritage points to the essential racism of an assimilationist culture. People who are marked as a racial Other are encouraged to transcend racial discrimination and prove themselves within the false universal proposed by the dominate culture. On so doing, the dominant culture points to the successfully assimilated as an example that others should follow. The fact that such success results in the erasure of the racialized Other's cultural difference is barely noticed by the dominant culture and never actually called into question as a violence perpetuated against people and their histories. I grew up in a family that, by all except for a few subtle indications, was white. There was very little in my growing-up environment that would have led me to question my status as an "American" fully entitled to all the possibilities of class and legitimate U.S. citizenship. By virtue of my family's class standing I had every reason to expect that I would be treated fairly within society and that my success or failure in life would have everything to do with my own ability and nothing to do with where I came from or the differences I represented to the dominant culture. I could take the social world for granted.

How is it, then, that questions about the social world, about race, class, gender, and sexuality, have come to define the very essence of my professional and personal adult life? The questions came about gradually, in the most veiled and barely perceptible ways. I could say that it began by asking questions of gender and sexuality, but that would not be entirely correct. It did not really *start* with questions of gender and sexuality, it was just that questions of gender and sexuality were easier and much safer to ask than questions of race or ethnicity. It was easy to find language to articulate questions of gender and sexuality; a "tomboy" growing up, I knew that I was not a typical girl. Tomboyishness simply gushed through my body. On a primordial level, the relation of my body to the world defied the norms and expectations for girls. It came naturally, without any reflection whatsoever, for me to challenge the notion that girls could not be tough or aggressive. Even still, my capacity for a critical gender consciousness was highly limited. I did generally assume that I was "normal" and would grow up to get married and have kids (wrong). I never questioned the fact that because I was a girl I did not have the same opportunities as athletically talented boys to pursue collegiate scholarships. Questions about ethnic and racial heritage, on the other hand, were far more complex and dangerous. Though not dark skinned, I have inherited subtle hints of my mestizo ancestry. I could look in the mirror as a young girl and see my almond-shaped brown eyes, high cheekbones, dark features, and the mestizo and Native American in my ancestry. Like so many U.S. Americans, my family was fond of making references to "the pure-blood Tennessee Cherokee" who was my grandfather's great-grandmother. I grew up making frequent visits to my maternal grandparents' home in Lucern Valley, in the desert of southern California. The desert has always been a magical place of unlimited beauty for me. I saw this as a child. It was my maternal grandmother who opened this view for me. And it is she who gets the credit for allowing me to look in the mirror as a child and see myself as not white. It was not that I considered myself Native American or Mexican in the cultural sense but simply that I knew I was not just a white person, that I had a heritage that was of a different world than my growing-up world. This was a difference that was not always perceptible to me and, even when perceptible, not clear-cut. Unlike my tomboyish gender identification, which I could prereflectively take for granted, my ethnic and racial identification led early on to conscious reflection that had no space for open consideration or acknowledgement. I had always had questions about my family heritage, yet there was no discourse available through which I could pursue those questions, only silence. Although I did not have a critical ethnic consciousness, questions about race and ethnicity comprised a constant backdrop against which I encountered the world.

So unavailable was the discourse to address questions of race, ethnicity, and class, and so heavy were the silences, that even during the mid-1970s, when the Los Angeles public school system instituted busing so that black inner-city kids could attend schools in the Valley, we had no way to talk about what was going on, much less actually interact with the new students at the school. Looking back on that time now, what is most glaringly apparent to me is that I cannot recall a single interpersonal or small-group conversation concerning anything having to do with black students being bused to our school. There were never any conversations in which we were invited to talk or listen to our peers talk about the experience of encountering each other. The black students were the Other, and by virtue of my not being one of them, I was white. There was never any context, formally in the materials we studied in class or informally by the way we interacted outside of class, to assist us in living through this encounter with different Others. There was a subtle and mostly unarticulated notion that busing was the right thing to do, and we did talk about how much of a sacrifice it was for the black kids to get up so early to ride the buses so far and then get home so late. Yet the strongest memory I have is of hearing a rumor one day that there was going to be a white-versus-black fight after school. The fight never materialized, but it is clear that talk of fighting was the only socially available language through which we could articulate the encounter with the black Others. It was not that our parents or the school officials explicitly told us that we should be antagonistic toward each other (perhaps some had) but that culturally and in the absence of any other discourse, the speech of *white-to-black* race relations is a speech of defending what is "ours," of fighting a dangerous enemy, of destroying the Other, of war. If there was a sense that it was right for the students to be bussed to our school, there was never any argument made as to why it was correct. No one broached the questions as to how the Los Angeles public school system had become segregated in the first place. There was no formal or informal consideration of the economic and political histories that result in urban racialization and ghettoization. I do not recall the history of race or ethnicity in the United States ever being a topic of study in my primary education. In the absence of these kinds of discourses, the white students simply responded with the racist attitudes carried in culture since the Europeans first set foot in the "new world." It is ironic that busing, seen as a partial remedy to the injustices perpetuated by racist attitudes and their accompanying racist institutional practices, becomes for the students living out the fact of busing policies, simply another place where racist divides are themselves perpetuated.

Yet an even greater personal irony came in my contact with other Mexican Americans in the Valley. I attended Chatsworth High School. Today, the name rings of the upward-mobility whiteness that dominated that place. It was through my high school softball team that I got my largest glimpse of those who bore the social markings of Mexican American. Our team traveled to various other high schools in the Valley, and playing at San Fernando High gave me my greatest exposure to the socially recognizable stereotypes that my family's class standing allowed us to escape. Traveling to San Fernando High forced me to ask questions about what it means to encounter people who were the more marked Mexican Americans, the ones who spoke Spanish, the low-riders, the girls with their big hair and white eyeliner, the guys with their hair slicked back and shirts buttoned only at the top, sharp and ironed all the way down—the ones who came from the barrios. I felt a vague sense of commonality with these marked others, yet I encountered them through a whole series of recognized differences having to do with class, lifestyle, and language. I did not know what zoot suit or *pocho* was. I knew they were different from me, but not in the same way that the black students were different. Unlike my experience with black students, I could not separate myself from the students I encountered at San Fernando High. I recall the time I was traveling with my summer league softball team to Arizona. The summer league teams were much more diverse in membership so that each team had players from all over the Valley. One of our players, Deede, was like the marked others I had encountered at San Fernando High. She was our pitcher and star player. Between games, several members of our team ended up in one of our motel rooms having a pillow fight. I cornered Deede, poised myself aggressively toward her, and pulled my pillow back in preparation for a full-force blow on her. Being fairly low on the hierarchy of this team, my cornering of Deede was quite a statement of presence and power. She looked startled but stopped my attack in its tracks by saying, "That's the Mexican in you." It was a moment that fueled the subtle recognition of my Mexican American ancestry that I had experienced all my life. It also coincided with the notion I developed through my maternal grandmother that there was a spiritual power to my ancestry connected to the desert and a certain kind of magical existence that transcended the ordinary facts of my day to day life. Yet, in all these encounters with Mexican Americans—seeing them on the street corners in Reseda and taking the school bus down to San Fernando High—I had no concrete way to pose questions about myself and them. What was my connection to them? What did these differences mean? Growing up in the environment I did, I had no way to actually ask those questions. I had no means of pursuing possible answers. Instead, they remained all around me, confronting me here and there like being tapped on the shoulder and turning to find no one there. Rooted as I was in that middle-class suburban white environment that dominated my southern California life, these questions seemed to have a life of hovering, never real, only surreal.

COMMUNICATION AND TRANSFORMATION IN PRAXIS

In this chapter and throughout the rest of this work, I rely heavily on descriptions of experience so as to engage in practice a methodological priority for traversing the complex terrain of the person as situated within history and culture. My aim is to trace through movements of consciousness that brings into relief the political and social implications of a person's experience and how that experience makes specific moments of being possible. In relying heavily on descriptions of my own experience, my purpose is not to offer a definitive statement on the experience of middle-class mixed-heritage Mexican Americans (whatever that might signify) or to suggest that my experiences of race and ethnicity provide the most informative ground from which to understand these concepts (my experience is not an exemplar but simply the example to which I am necessarily tied). Were I to do so, I would be taking for granted the fact that my capacity to describe these very experiences is itself produced by my particular location in social space and time. The meaningfulness I come to make of race and ethnicity in my life must be understood as the conjunction between my taking up of representations made available (and unavailable) to me via the dominant culture and my embodied experience of those representations, which itself produces its own representations of race and ethnicity.

Because being-in-communication-with is an extricable fact of human existence, the study of race and ethnicity requires that one take up the specifics of lived experience as it emerges from and engages the anonymity of the social and historical world. Studying the experience of Chicanos, Chicanas, and Chicana lesbians resonates strongly with my own personal experience. Yet it also identifies gaps where I recognize distance between myself and many of the Chicanas and Chicanos whose work I have read and whose lives I have learned about. Recognizing that distance, however, also creates the possibility for making connections with our points of commonality while reducing the risk of ignoring or underestimating the importance of our differences. Mexican Americans constitute a widely diverse community. Respecting the differences among us while attending to the common circumstances of history and the racist practices of the dominant culture allows for authentic communication that can interrogate its own conditions of possibility and thus also the possibility for truly liberatory practices. Because of my engagement with the lives and work of Chicanas and Chicanos, I have been able to recognize the facticity of my familial heritage in ways that I could have never done except by virtue of that engagement. In this way, the cloak of questions and uncertainties that I have carried preconsciously all my life begins to recede as I engage the samenesses and differences I discover.

It was the gap between the passionate connection I found in Chicana feminism and the ambiguities of my actual living world that ultimately made the terrain covered in this work available to me. This gap also made it possible for me to recognize the significance of certain facts of my life that the Anglo culture would not have allowed me to recognize. I discovered a nonstationary critical consciousness—a critical consciousness that could take neither its critical impulse nor its content for granted. In a similar way, I came to recognize the differences in generational perspectives between my grandmother, father, and myself and how assimilation must be understood as a very different question for each of us. It therefore becomes possible throughout to recognize the necessity of linking a race-critical (and gender-critical and sexuality-critical and class-critical) consciousness with the sometimes dangerous tendencies carried in the cool, distanced, and purely academic engagement. The theoretical effort is necessarily distanced from the chaotic, confusing, and often contradictory immediacy of experience. The theoretical effort, therefore, can also be coldly detached from our fleshy rootedness in the world. Theorizing for the sake of theorizing can itself be a strategy of evasion, delusion, and willful ignorance. Despite these dangerous tendencies of portending liberatory practice in a detached theoretical effort, we need theory to develop more powerful and sophisticated tools for engaging the fleshy rootedness of human-world existence. The challenge (and responsibility) lies in bridging the gap between those theoretical tools and our flesh, putting them concretely to the lived experiences through which it has been possible for us to speak, hear, see, feel, and do in the first place. It is, of course, the courageous work of Chicana feminists who have paved the way for me to travel this path that tends to reveal itself to me only after having gone down it.

The remainder of this text continues to traverse various gaps within my own experience and understanding as they have developed through an examination of my own lived experience, the history of Chicanas, and the application of semiotic and existential phenomenology. Taking seriously the fact of lived experience as an essential aspect of antiracist and antisexist liberatory work requires that the liberation theorist put her abstract claims into concrete practice. Chapter two, "Speaking as a Chicana: Tracing Cultural Heritage through Silence and Betrayal," aims to do just that by tracing through the movements of my own consciousness awareness relative to my coming to speak as a Chicana. Because liberation can never be achieved abstractly, it is incumbent on those portending liberatory practice to actualize that practice concretely and materially. Although such an effort makes its achievement of liberation primarily for practitioner herself, it is a necessary starting point from which liberatory achievements may be made on a broader scale—a point particularly important for building alliances across communities that have born different degrees of racist, sexist, and homophobic attack presently and through history. Taking account of who we are and how we come (noetically) to seek alliances in antiracist, antisexist, and antihomophobic (noematic) practices provides a basis from which we can build real and functioning bridges between and among people of different backgrounds and experience. In this way, broader achievements of liberation are made possible by making critical and creative linkages across time and space—across generations of persons who have shared a common space (land or history) and among those who share the same time across many spaces. Chapter two takes account of the psychic and corporeal terrain on which I have traveled in coming to consciousness as a Chicana. Largely autobiographical, this chapter offers an account of the progressive and spiraling movement between and among what I identify as three distinct modes of consciousness through which I have moved and am still moving relative to my Chicana identity. Each of these modes of consciousness entails different and evolving relationships between myself, my father, his parents, and the legacies of culture and history. In taking this account, I foreground the present of my lifetime, engaging the past so as to make sense of experiences of the present.

Chapter three, "Radical Ambiguities and the Chicana Lesbian: Body Topographies on Contested Lands," works in a slightly different way. By foregrounding contemporary Chicana feminist and Chicana lesbian readings of the history of the land that is today northern Mexico and the southwestern United States, this chapter seeks to account for historical movement through which the Chicana lesbian comes to emerge as a site for transformative praxis. This chapter interrogates the Chicana lesbian as a site of radical ambiguity that is traceable to the whole of the struggle engage by generations of native women, mestizas, and Mexicanas ever since the first encounter with the Spanish imperialists. Reading the history of this land via the struggles engaged by native women, mestizas, and Mexicanas problematizes the "assimilationist versus nationalist" and "complicitous-traitor versus loyal-culturalist" binarisms that have tended to constrain generations of racialized women struggling against various forms of oppression. By examining the radical ambiguity embodied by the contemporary "Chicana lesbian," this chapter suggests different possibilities for understanding and achieving radical transformation for both the person and the social world. Chapter four, "*La Conciencia de la Mestiza*: Intra- and Intersubjective Transformations of Racist and Homophobic Culture," examines how the recognition of oppression in concrete form and as lived corporeally on the body functions as a prerequisite for freeing oneself from the internalization of that oppression. Looking at the intrasubjective experience of the mestiza engaging a *mestizaje* practice, this chapter takes Gloria Anzaldúa's description of *la conciencia de la mestiza* as a thematic guide in the analysis of transformational praxis. It focuses on sexual and ethnic oppressions and identifies a nexus of intersecting pressures that create certain boundaries and thus also certain possibilities for the emergence of different kinds of conscious awareness and transformations in the material, communicative, and intersubjective worlds within which all human beings are situated. Chapter five, "Chicana Feminism and Struggle in the Flesh: Racist Assimilation and Cultural Recovery," returns to a cross-generational consideration of struggles engaged by Chicanas and Chicana lesbians and seeks to understand how the dominating forces of cultural assimilation lead to different strategies for counteracting the erasures produced by those forces of cultural assimilation. This chapter specifically takes up the question as to how we might go forward after the fact of cultural loss. If we recognize that the past can never be what it was again, that the assimilationist forces have already worked their way into our preconscious and taken-for-granted ways of apprehending the world, then how do we go forward with an antiassimilationist effort? What does it mean to recover a cultural heritage when important aspects of the cultural heritage could be irrecoverable? Finally, chapter six, "Chicana y Chicana: A Dialogue on Race, Class and Chicana Identity," is the product of two academic feminists exploring with each other our processes of coming to consciousness as Chicanas and our political and personal consciousness regarding the racism and classism that has contextualized the development of our ethnic identities. The dialogic form of this chapter allows the reader to see the complex sets of similarities and differences between us as two academic feminists who share a common cultural heritage. I conclude the work with this dialogue to reemphasize the praxis thus engaged. No matter how carefully and precisely I endeavor to detail the contours of history and experience that make different moments of consciousness possible, there will always be something important left out—and this must necessarily be so. There is something entirely ineffable about being-in-communication-with. The dialogic form of this last chapter implies in its very form all the liveliness entailed in the immediacy of exchange that can never be fully accounted for—an appropriate place for this work to end.

NOTES

1. See Langellier (1989) for an excellent discussion of the theoretical, methodological, and political issues that distinguish different approaches to the use of narratives in research.

2. See also Butler (1993, 27–53) for a discussion of exclusion as the necessary outside that must be recognized as always present in the theoretical effort.

3. See Takaki (1993) for an important discussion of the differences in the ease of assimilation for various immigrant groups in the United States.

4. I am not aware of any other work in the area of Chicana feminism that takes up semiotic and existential phenomenology explicitly as a philosophical and applied approach. There are, however, many Chicana feminist works that take up

key philosophical and applied aspects that are consonant with semiotic and existential phenomenology. These points are identified and developed throughout the text. There is a substantial body of work combining feminist theory and philosophy with semiotic and existential phenomenology. De Beauvoir's *The Second Sex* (1989) is in all likelihood the first existential and phenomenological examination of women's situation. See also Allen and Young (1989), Young (1984, 1990), Bartky (1990), Allen (1983), Butler (1986, 1989, 1990), and Langellier (1994).

5. Thank you to Patricia Corey for pointing me to this quotation and to the students in "Semiotic Phenomenology" (spring 1999) for our close reading of Sobchack.

6. For discussions of Chicana feminism as a field and/or body of work, see Galindo and Gonzales (1999), Trujillo (1991, 1998), García (1997), Córdova (1994), Rebolledo and Rivero (1983), de la Torre and Pesquera (1993), Zavella (1987), López (1993), Hererra-Sobek and Viramontes (1988), Alarcón et al. (1993), Sánchez (1985), and Castillo (1994).

7. "Manner or style of thinking" is, of course, taken from Merleau-Ponty's famous preface to *Phenomenology of Perception* (1986, viii).

8. On habit, see de Lauretis (1984, 174) and Peirce (1958, 5.538); on habitus, see Bourdieu (1977) and Lanigan (1992, 159); on communicative praxis, see Schrag (1986).

9. When I use the term *parameters,* I mean for it to signify an openness that includes the relation between system and boundary, rules/relations, and objects.

10. See MacKinnon (1987, 32–45) for a discussion of the same dynamic with regard to gender difference.

11. See Gordon (1995a) and Sedgwick (1990). See Gordon (1997, 73–88) for discussion of a racial and sexual matrix whereby racism is necessarily misogynist and homophobic.

12. See Ihde (1986, 44–54) for a concise discussion of the shift from transcendental phenomenology in the Husserlian tradition to the existential turn in phenomenology exemplified in the work of Heidegger and Merleau-Ponty.

13. See also Merleau-Ponty (1986) and Lanigan (1991).

14. In this sense, the present work differs radically from Richard Rodriguez's *Hunger of Memory* (1982). Taking his own experience as subject matter and exemplar, Rodriguez offers an introspective and self-centered account of an ethnic other who seeks and gains a self-alienated entrance to the "mainstream" of U.S. American society.

15. Fanon (1967) makes this point abundantly clear. See also Spitzack (1988) for an excellent illustration of this dynamic with regard to white middle-class women's body image.

16. An example of what Gordon (1995a) identifies as the bad faith of antiblack racism.

17. This is the basis of the arguments made in favor of feminist standpoint epistemologies. See Harding (1986, 1991), Hill Collins (1986), and Hartsock (1983). While the second wave of feminism helped give rise to the popularity of standpoint epistemologies, acknowledgment must go to earlier advocates for social change whose own insights preceded the academic rise of these general ideas. See Córdova (1994) and Guy-Sheftall (1995, 23–142) for a discussion of this with regard

to the early Chicana and African American feminists. For an excellent critique of feminist standpoint epistemologies, see Bar On (1993).

18. In the late 1970s and early 1980s, the Valley became especially well known for the "Valley Girl" stereotype. "Valley Girls" were known for a particular style of speech ("for sure, for sure") dress, and social habits. Chief among theses social habits was frequenting of the Galleria, a large upscale shopping mall located just off of Sepulveda and Ventura Boulevards at the southeast corner of the Valley. It was a stereotype whose signification was entirely white upper-middle-class female. For Chicanos and Chicanas of the southwestern United States, however, "the Valley" has at least two very different significations with radically different histories. One is connected to the San Joaquin Valley in central California and the other to the Rio Grande Valley in southern Texas.

2

SPEAKING AS A CHICANA:
TRACING CULTURAL HERITAGE THROUGH
SILENCE AND BETRAYAL

I knew that then, sitting in the Oakland auditorium (as I know in my poetry), that the only thing worth writing about is what seems to be unknown and, therefore, fearful.

—Cherríe Moraga

In our self-reflexivity and in our active participation with the issues that confront us, whether it be through writing, front-line activism, or individual self-development, we are also uncovering the inter-faces, the very spaces and places where our multiple-surfaced, colored, racially gendered bodies intersect and interconnect.

—Gloria Anzaldúa

How does one begin addressing issues that for most of one's life have been shrouded in silence and so unavailable that they could not have been formulated explicitly? Reaching back through generations of a racist-assimilationist culture puts many people in this position. I argued in chapter one that racist-assimilationist forces have been and continue to be a pervasive force in the development of contemporary U.S. American culture. These forces direct many people and families toward survival strategies that tend to replicate and reinforce "success" in terms of racist assimilation and its whitewashed sense of normalcy and achievement. Identifying how the racist-assimilationist forces of culture function across generations and in one's familial life is a first step to counteracting them. Yet that identification is difficult because the effect of racist assimilation is the erasure of difference whereby one may detect and engage boundaries making culture recognizable. Taking up the effort to shift through erasures of culture and history is never easy or self-apparent. It is an endeavor fraught with ambiguity, fearfulness, and even terror as one interrogates the relations of self-to-family-to-history-to-culture that have been the very formation of the self-as-recognized and now challenged. Our effort in developing liberatory theory and praxis must begin here, by putting into

33

concrete practice an interrogation of those very terms in which our selves-as-recognized are called into question.

Mexican Americans constitute one of the largest minority groups in the United States. Yet only a portion of us ever comes to designate ourselves as Chicano or Chicana. What makes the difference between those who come to take up the Chicano or Chicana label as a politically driven designator of self and those who do not? On what terms can we say that the taking up of the Chicano or Chicana label as a designator of self does or does not participate in a liberatory effort? If being Mexican American is insufficient to identify oneself in terms of a Chicano or Chicana based political struggle, then what is? How are we to understand the relationship between the objective conditions of a life (say, working-class Mexican American) and the motivation to make a judgment that leads one to say, "I am a Chicana"? Merleau-Ponty's (1986) answer is instructive:

> What makes me a proletarian [Chicana] is not the economic [racial] system or society considered as systems of impersonal forces, but these institutions [racialized knowledges] as I carry them within me and experience them; nor is it an intellectual operation devoid of motive, but my way of being in the world with this institutional framework. (443)

Following Merleau-Ponty, we can say that what makes the difference is the very way in which we carry the racialized knowledge and institutional frameworks that make "Mexican American" tacitly understood as a *neutral* designator of persons.[1] As long as we remain locked within the social momentum of racist assimilation, we will live unconsciously within racialized designators supplied by that momentum. As we live through the ambiguity of our intersubjective subjectivity—of our being-in-communication-with—we have the potentiality of tending toward both maintaining the tacitly understood designations of ourselves and questioning them. As we live within the ambiguity of our social becoming, we may, within the balance of our reaching toward a future, come to question those tacitly understood designators. The more strongly we recognize and engage our own questioning of those tacitly understood designators, the more we recognize a difference between who we are and who the dominant culture would encourage us to become. Once we begin calling into question the terms of our cultural becoming, a certain "magnetic field" emerges in our social space whereby it is possible that we come to perceive concretely the costs endured as a result of normative forces of racist assimilation. In this process, the person comes to experience, in their very perception of the world, the racialization of persons and groups as a "common obstacle to the existence of each and every one" of us (Merleau-Ponty 1986, 445). Now, the tacitly accepted designators of self and social world become understood as insufficient and therefore in need of a new struggle-based and nonneutral designator of self: Chicano or Chicana. Thus, we understand the process of coming to speak as a Chicana not simply as a decision to do so but rather as a coming to perceive concretely one's own self-in-relation-to-others and the world as fundamentally different than one had previously.

Coming to understand the apparently neutral designator, Mexican American, as insufficient is not merely something that happens in a moment. There may be a moment at which I consciously question the adequacy of the assumed label for the first time, but that moment was preceded by moments of preconscious questioning and followed by post-conscious rethinking (and reexperiencing) of the whole of one's life. As Merleau-Ponty (1986) puts it, "The revolutionary movement, like the work of the artist, is an intention which itself creates its instruments and its means of expression. The revolutionary project is not the result of a deliberate judgement, or the explicit positing of an end" (445). In this way we understand the moment of coming to speak as a Chicana is a moment preceded by a maturation "in co-existence before bursting forth into words and being related to objective ends" (446). What had been a noetic disposition becomes a noematic content of conscious awareness. Once this happens, a whole range of noetic dispositions occurring over the entirety of one's life may be made noematic, which itself is made possible by a new noetic disposition.[2] Interrogating this shifting of noetic and noematic correlations gives us reflexive access to the very parameters of the social and discursive world through which we come to feel what we feel, think what we think, speak what we speak, and do what we do. Taking up that access changes us—one can never go back to the tacit nonconsciousness that preceded the making explicit to oneself the questions that had been shrouded in silence. It is precisely this effort that is exemplified in the fleshy, bold, and courageous work of many Chicanas and Chicana lesbians. Recognizing the importance of this work requires an equally fleshy, bold, and courageous effort by each of us. It is a mode of interrogation based on an immersion in the ambiguities and struggles of the present, where a looking back and shifting through allows one to resignify the significance of experience and event. In taking up this effort, we need the apparently linear passage of time to be able to look back and see. Having done so, however, the present and possible futures necessarily change. This is not a merely cyclical process with its own teleology but a spiraling action whereby the present changes the past, the past changes the present, and in every case the possibility of the future remains open, ambiguous, and affected by the ongoing spiraling that is the present. My effort in this chapter is to map out, as dynamically as possible, this spiraling of present, past, and future with a hope that the work thus gives us adequately fleshed out descriptions (already a critical interpretation) of experience through which we may better understand and engage processes of deassimilation.

IDENTIFYING MODES OF ETHNIC CONSCIOUSNESS

Reflecting strictly on the processes involved in my coming to speak as a Chicana, I can identify three distinct modes of (noetic) consciousness that define major shifts in my thinking, feeling, and acting (noema) in relation to myself, my family, and the many students and colleagues of color (both gay and straight) in the academy whom I have had the privilege of knowing and working with over the course of my academic career. The first mode of consciousness is an *unknowing-knowing*.[3] This mode of consciousness was dominant throughout my childhood and up until about the age of twenty-three, when I began attending California State University at Northridge.[4] It was at Cal State Northridge that I first sought connection with a group of Chicano students, but then, it was not that I really *sought them out*. Because of my Spanish surname, I received all the campus mailers targeted toward the Mexican American student body. Receiving those mailers and recognizing that others recognized me—albeit anonymously—led me to begin searching among my Mexican American peers for points of contact and commonality. Prior to seeking out those contacts and commonalities, I *knew* I had Mexican American ancestry from my father, but my family's fairly affluent southern California lifestyle made the knowledge of my Mexican American heritage, something *unknown,* remain irrelevant—a message I got from my father. This unknowing-knowing mode of consciousness encourages assimilation. If one remains oriented toward cultural ancestry as an unknowing-knowing, the forces of assimilation will continue to wear their way through the very perceptual possibilities of a person's living world. Over time (generations) any possible knowledge of cultural heritage will be simply lost. Assimilation will have reached its logical end and will transform into the more general forces of social and cultural normalization that maintain the exclusions that allow racist knowledge to be perpetuated as culture.

The second mode of consciousness is a *preknowing-knowing,* and it emerged as I began looking for connections with my peers and asking barely conscious questions, entirely of myself, about what exactly my relationship was to Chicanos/as, Mexican Americans, and Spanish-speaking people generally.[5] Finding myself targeted as a Mexican American through those campus mailers allowed me to begin *broaching* these questions to myself. Even still, I had no clear idea of where to go to find answers—or even that answers could be possible. Questions concerning ethnic and cultural heritage still hovered about me without my being able to fully grasp them. When I first began showing up at the Chicano Students Association meeting at the university, I was not yet involved in explicitly engaging questions about my family's history or our ethnic heritage. But as soon as I began participating, I did ask myself if I belonged there. It was natural, and without any conscious decision on my part, to look to see if the Chicano students seemed to think I belonged there. There were, of course, many awkward moments when I became all too self-conscious about speech, language, gesture, clothing, appearance, and so on. I felt generally welcomed, yet seeing the differences carried primarily in my economic class standing left me feeling like I did not really belong with Chicanos and Chicanas. However tentative those first efforts to consciously seek out my Mexican American peers were, they gave me enough of a feeling of possibility that I could continue broaching—even if not fully engaging—questions about my ethnic and cultural heritage. This second mode of consciousness, a preknowing-knowing, has a particular precariousness about it; it is situated in the realm of the preconscious, where there is a reverberation back and forth between what is unknown but sensed as a possible knowing and what is known. It is a mode of consciousness marked by ambiguity and uncertainty, and, therefore, possibility and danger.

The third mode of consciousness regarding my Chicana identity is a *knowing-unknown*, where one knows precisely that there is a field of unknowingness that is directly relevant to oneself. It involves an *explicit asking of questions*, first of myself and my family history and then of the history of the Chicano people—especially those whose histories lie on the land of the southwestern United States. It is on this land that acts of oppression and blatant racism have defined the struggle for survival of the native and mestizo people. Entering this mode of consciousness coincided with efforts at formal and informal education where I began reading about the histories of various sorts of oppressions and efforts at liberation. I also began seeking out other Chicanas and women of color in an effort to find common points of identification. As I began searching to learn all that I had not known, I looked especially to Chicana lesbians and Chicana feminists. What I found was a language about and disposition toward life as a fleshy, messy, bodied experience. Borders that I had been raised to never see were engaged directly, passionately, courageously. Dichotomies that had allowed me to maintain the notion of an essential and irrevocable difference between me and the Other Mexican Americans who were not like me were attacked. It was from here, from engaging these kinds of work by Chicana lesbians, lesbians, and feminists of color, that I could begin to trace back through a life and come to speak for myself as a Chicana.

These three modes of consciousness are not separate but rather share overlapping boundaries. My movement between and among them is necessarily progressive and spiraling. In order to adequately account for the progressive and spiraling movement among these modes of consciousness, it is important to privilege the overlapping boundaries as they lead to specific moments of conscious experience that can be identified as one or another of the modes of consciousness I have described previously. Although each mode of consciousness overlaps with the others, they have areas of distinction among them. Identifying their distinctions in addition to their overlap is also very important. The three modes are (1) unknowing-knowing, (2) preknowing-knowing, and (3) knowing-unknown. The difference between modes one and two is the degree to which questions about one's familial, ethnic, and cultural heritage can be broached in the preconsciousness of lived experience. Movement from mode one to mode two entails a shift from a subtle and *barely accessible* sense that ethnic, racial, and cultural heritage is important to who I am to a *recognition*, sometimes fleeting, that ethnic, racial, and cultural heritage is important to who I am and who I might become. Both of these modes of conscious are as dynamic as the moment-by-moment shifting of conscious awareness in experience. In other words, the shift from unknowing to preknowing occurs dynamically from one moment to the next. Only when a certain preponderance of preknowingness takes hold is it possible that the second mode of consciousness may shift into the third mode of consciousness. Otherwise, the preknowing moves back into the unknowing as one simply moves through the mundane of everyday life. As the preknowingness takes stronger hold, however, questions about one's ethnic, racial, and cultural heritage can be posed explicitly to oneself. Now what could have been comfortably avoided is confronted as ambiguous and not necessarily answerable questions about oneself. One becomes aware that in knowing what one knows, there is also something vastly unknown.

Movement through these three modes of consciousness begins with an *unknowing*-as-knowing and ends in a knowing-that-there-is-an-*unknown*. The difference between the active "unknowing" to the static "unknown" is very important. On reaching the third mode of consciousness, one recognizes the objective and static fact that one is to varying degrees ignorant of one's own history and possibility. This ignorance is the logical outcome of a racist-assimilationist culture. Knowing that there is an unknown that is perpetuated within the very terms of our social and cultural existence leads one to pose explicit questions about one's history and the circumstances of culture that result in the ignorances one recognizes in oneself. On posing those questions explicitly, one may engage an effort of recovery where one can begin to imagine a future differently than one had previously. There is a danger, however, in stopping at this third mode of consciousness because it can slide into a mode not only of knowing that there is the unknown but of thinking that one *knows what is un-*

known. Should one remain fully located within this mode of consciousness, one will undoubtedly posit a liberatory effort as simply enacting what
one knows should be enacted. Although one may continue to pose questions about history and culture because, as it were, one can never learn
too much, this mode of consciousness can also close down any interrogation of the unknowing and preknowing that opened the possibilities for
the recognition of the unknown in the first place. Thus, the third mode
of consciousness must lead one back to the first mode of consciousness
in a continuous spiraling movement. Our liberatory praxis must return
again to the first and second modes of consciousness in order to avoid the
easy slip into an arrogantly assumed *knowing what is unknown* and therefore must be addressed for liberation. What follows is an account of the
progressive and spiraling movement between and among these three
modes of consciousness in my own experience—it takes account of the
very terrain on which I have come to consciousness as a Chicana.[6]

ENTERING INTO A CHICANA LESBIAN WORLD: SORTING THROUGH THE PREKNOWING-KNOWING

Coming to consciousness as a Chicana has been, for me, intricately
connected with my coming to consciousness as a lesbian.[7] The knowledge
produced by coming out to myself as a lesbian was transformative for me
personally; it also revealed to me the ways in which culture and social discourse can literally preclude knowledge and understanding (as unknowing) that is central to our very existence as particular human beings. Coming out as a lesbian at the age of twenty-two revealed to me the ways in
which culture can directly oppress people deep within their own psychic
being.

Like many other gay and lesbian people, once I came out, I could look
back on the whole of my life and see the ways in which I had always been
a lesbian but had never been allowed the space to actually live and consciously experience that part of myself. So I began to broach barely conscious questions to myself: If the oppressions of culture have prevented
me from seeing important aspects of sexuality, then how have the oppressions of culture prevented me from seeing important aspects of my
ethnicity? My explorations into feminist theory had allowed me to understand that because cultural norms made heterosexuality compulsory (Rich
1993), certain power relations between men and women were reinforced
within culture. So I knew that by presenting ethnic heritage as secondary
to "American" (white) identity, certain power relations between darkness
and lightness were maintained. Yet the apparent insignificance of my
Mexican American heritage created an important difference for me

between coming to consciousness as a lesbian and coming to consciousness as a Chicana: Whereas there was very little ambiguity for me about my lesbian self, I was filled with nothing but ambiguity about my Chicana self. The ambiguities of my Chicana identity situated me firmly within the second mode of consciousness, a preknowing-knowing, a mode of asking barely conscious questions entirely to myself about the ambiguities of my life, my history, and my possible futures.

Entering into a new consciousness-of-self via certitude versus ambiguity made an important difference. It made a difference because having certitude generally discourages asking questions about that which is certain. Having ambiguity, on the other hand, provokes questions. The ambiguities of my Chicana identity propelled me, first and foremost, into questions about my father and his life and, second, into the relationship between social location and ethnic identity and the circumstances of sociocultural powers and privileges that are distributed according to the perceptible signs of a person's ethnic identity. Because my father kept his own life history largely inaccessible to me, questions and uncertainty predominated in my early development of Chicana identity. The description I offer in the following paragraphs illustrates how I processed this concern by separating out my lesbian certainty from my Chicana ambiguity. I illustrate this point concretely by comparing my experiences coming to consciousness as a lesbian and a Chicana.

Although I have always been entrenched within the heterosexism that is pervasive throughout contemporary U.S. American culture, there was a certain point at which a number of circumstances converged to create an explosion of certainty whereby I knew that the people and the world were wrong in assuming that I was heterosexual and that I was at varying degrees of risk in revealing the error of heterosexual presumption. Thus began a struggle in which, as a normal feature of my daily life, I had to consciously consider how, when, and to what degree to control my expressions as a lesbian. Early on in the coming-out process, simple things like switching pronouns so that it was obvious that I was talking about a female-female intimate couple were major markers of being out. With heterosexual friends, topics about couples, dating, or the attractiveness of a member of the opposite sex presented particular challenges. Simply going along with the conversation would make one tacitly pass as heterosexual. In these cases, commenting on the attractiveness of another woman or the predicaments of a lesbian relationship constituted a coming out— albeit a comment that usually made for moments of awkward adjustment in the flow of the conversation. As I became more comfortable with my lesbian identity among my heterosexual friends and acquaintances, it became easier to simply be my lesbian self without either blending into heterosexual assumption or having to force "lesbian" topics for conversation.

Yet every instance of "coming out" or simply carrying my lesbian self openly always carries the knowledge that such acts of coming out involve very real risks. These risks range from simple rejection to outward disdain and even outright violence. On coming out, I began what is a lifelong predicament of dealing with the gay closet in a heterosexist culture.

My conscious struggles with ethnic identity have been, like my conscious struggles with sexual identity, a feature primarily of my adult life. I am not sure what prompted me to respond to those campus mailers and seek out Chicano students as a twenty-three-year-old undergraduate. Perhaps it was that in coming out as a lesbian I sensed vast areas of discovery waiting out there for me. Perhaps coming out as a lesbian emboldened me enough to seek out other aspects of myself and chart my own way in life. I do not remember consciously deciding to seek out Chicanos/as. I do remember attending their meetings and their dances and feeling terribly excited and a little out of place. But I must say that in the twelve or so years since I first began tentatively seeking out Chicanos/as and other people of color, I have felt welcomed and never challenged about the "authenticity" of my ethnic standing. In fact, I have often had the experience of being looked to by Chicano and Chicana students for guidance and advice. When I was a new assistant professor at a small private college in the Boston area, I received an invitation to the 1993 Harvard-Radcliffe Raza Pachanga at Harvard University (sponsored by the East Coast Chicano Students Association). Accepting that invitation put me in the position of being one of several Chicano/Latino professors and community activists presenting work to nearly 100 Chicano students over a three-day period. The vast majority of these students were from Texas, California, and other western states. It was my first presentation ever to a group gathered under the Chicano/Latino label. My presentation was early in the program, and I talked about confronting the ambiguity of my ethnic and cultural heritage. It was a theme that seemed to strike a chord with many of the students. Over the next few days I had many conversations with the students and other Pachanga participants. The students asked me for advice and about my experiences in the academy. I saw them searching through their own experience and working to chart their own way in life. In every academic institution I have worked, my surname has signaled a possibility of connection and support for brown, black, and other racially or ethnically marked persons. In every academic institution I have worked, students have approached me with a hope that the possibilities for support and recognition identified by the fact of my surname might become a reality. That I have been able to provide that recognition and support is one of my proudest achievements as an academic professional. However ambiguous my ethnic standing may be, I have come to realize that it has been primarily among Anglos that my Mexican American cultural heritage could be erased—that I could fail their ethnic test. In the beginning, however, I did not need others to question my ethnic identity because I was very busy questioning it for myself.

Early in my graduate work, I sought out feminist theory primarily to help me understand more about what I knew was my lesbian self. As I studied feminist texts, I encountered discussions of racism and classism. Works by Baca Zinn, Webber Cannon, Higginbotham, and Thornton Dill (1986), Gonzales (1977), Zavella (1987), and Moraga and Anzaldúa (1983) were especially important during this time. Moraga and Anzaldúa's work, along with Audre Lorde's (1984) work, was crucially important in helping me make connections between the experiences of Chicana and other women of color. García's (1989) essay was important in helping me to make connections with African American, Asian American, and Native American women. I began to see these questions of racism and classism within feminist theory as having relevance to my own life. I was already in graduate school by this time, studying the philosophy of communication.[8] It was 1986, I was twenty-six years old, and I was in the Department of Speech Communication at Southern Illinois University. Moving to the Midwest from southern California was a culture shock, to say the least. Adjusting to life in the Midwest provided another layer of experiences and feelings for me to grapple with. I went to graduate school because I felt it would allow me to continue to pursue the journey of self-discovery that was initiated by my coming out as a lesbian.

During the initial stages of finding relevance in issues of race and ethnicity, I generally maintained silence regarding my developing ethnic identity: I was very cautious about seeking out other Chicanas, other Chicana lesbians, or other women of color. Being a graduate student and living in southern Illinois made it difficult for me to actively pursue connections with Chicanas, Latinas, and other people of color. There were no other Chicanas or Latinas in my graduate program.[9] I did participate in the black students' protest against the downsizing of the African American Studies program. I also did volunteer work at the battered women's shelter, but whatever Chicana or Latina community was there was beyond my perception as I struggled to figure out how graduate school worked, how to form new relationships, and how to be out as a lesbian. Whereas I could carry my lesbian self fairly openly (and therefore confront issues of homophobia, heterosexism, and so on), I did not feel any openness about my ethnic self. I could move about in my everyday world without having questions about my ethnic identity provoked by myself or others.

Unlike my experience as a lesbian, I rarely felt myself in a position of having to consciously consider how, when, and to what degree to control any conscious expression of my ethnic identity. If there were any cases where persons stereotyped me on the basis of my dark hair and facial features (on light brown skin), almond-shaped eyes, and high "Indian" cheekbones, I was oblivious to it. Unlike my sexual identity, I did not, at this time, experience my ethnic identity as problematic within the normal conditions of everyday life. My recognition of racism within feminism fueled my own questions about my ethnic identity and helped create conditions that moved me more consciously into my own ambiguities regarding my ethnic identity. My internal questions about my ethnic identity came more and more to occupy my conscious thinking and feeling. But still, it was not until I received my doctoral degree and had my first tenure-track position that I began writing about my Chicana identity.

The difference between the certitude I carried within my sexual identity and the ambiguity I carried within my ethnic identity had a lot to do with the concreteness of the human body and the way it carries out perception and expression. Once I came out to myself as a lesbian, I realized that I had been ignorant about my sexuality. But after having come out, I never felt ignorant about my sexual identity. I have often, on the other hand, felt an ignorance about my ethnic identity—although I have, ironically, come to know more about Mexican American history than gay history. The difference, I think, lies in the fact that I experience my lesbian sexuality concretely in my own body. My ethnic body, in contrast, has never been tied to the concreteness of speaking Spanish—a fact I regret immensely but over which I had no control as a child. Since coming out as a lesbian, I have often looked in the mirror and wondered how people looking at me could not know that I am not straight. I have always carried myself in a fairly "butch" way and prefer masculine to feminine clothing. Living as an "out" lesbian meant seeing the butchiness that I present to the world as revealing of my lesbian self. In this way, the human body is a sign that signifies both to myself and to others (and as my perception of their perception of me). Coming out as a lesbian allowed me to see the code of my own lesbian self as it had organized much of my bodily style throughout my life. Once I came out as a lesbian, I knew that my body spoke the language of lesbian sexuality; there was absolutely no question about my standing as a lesbian.

There is, of course, an important parallel to the process of coming to see the ethnicness one presents to the world. For Mexican Americans, Spanish is a primary code through which ethnicness is carried out. A young child growing up in Texas during the 1930s, for example, might have received the message that the Spanish language through which his body communicated naturally to the world was a "bad" language that signified ignorance and low social standing. If Spanish was the home language, the child must then distance himself from the linguistic code that had been most intimately connected to the self. As the child internalizes the racist message about his home language, he seeks to distance himself from the formal linguistic code (Spanish) and all the tonalities, rhythms, and corporealities carried out in speaking the language that is his most intimate contact with the world. Should the child continue down this road in developing his capacity for human expression, the tonalities, rhythms, and corporealities of spoken English will come to dominate, and thus the child's connection to cultural patterns carried out in the Spanish language diminishes. Assimilation becomes inevitable. Should the child, at some later point in his life, consciously reject the dominant culture's message about his home language, he might embrace Spanish and come to see his speaking in Spanish as a way of embracing an ethnic self that the dominant culture would have preferred to remain assimilated. In the moment of embracing the language that he had learned to distance himself from, a new possibility for seeing one's self and body as an ethnic self and body emerges. Such a person might look in the mirror or listen to himself speak in Spanish and wonder how anyone, including himself, could deny the ethnicness of his body.

It has taken a long time for me to come to see and feel my own body as an ethnic body. Absent the capacity to express myself in Spanish, I am left to reach for less tangible traces of an ethnic self that have been buried under layers of assimilation into Anglo culture and practice. The fact that I have spent so much of my adult and professional life occupied with questions about my "ethnic self" and my familial-cultural heritage becomes a primary signifier of this ethnic self of mine. It is a signifier that, although it lacks the obvious concreteness of experiencing one's own sexuality or speaking Spanish, retains the general concreteness of human perception. There is, for example, the experience of looking into the mirror and the faces of others. I remember when I first began speaking about my struggles with my ethnic identity. Linda Alcoff, a Latina colleague, reminded me about "the politics of the visible" and suggested that I looked more ethnic than she did—a fact that certainly made a difference in others' perception of me. The next time I looked in the mirror, I saw my dark features and wondered what I had been seeing when I looked in the mirror previously. I remembered my maternal grandmother and how she had encouraged me to see the Indian in myself. Thus began a process in which I have learned (again) to *see myself seeing* into my own face and the faces of others and see more than white or black; it is a searching for subtleties and complexities that Anglo cultural perception denies. Yet still there is a profoundly important way in which, until this body of mine can speak in Spanish, gesture in a "Spanishly" way, and be immersed in Spanish-speaking communities, there will remain ambiguities about its ethnic identification.[10] There is a crucially important difference, it seems, between rebuking Anglo culture from within the linguistic code of that culture and being immersed within the fundamentally different cultural codes carried with the language of the different and subjugated culture. This is not to say, however, that because one does speak Spanish that one necessarily has the capacity to challenge the terms of a racist-assimilationist culture. My experiences with a wide variety of students of color in common struggles against erasure and nonrecognition suggest that usurping the effects of a racist-assimilationist culture requires a many-sided attack that cannot be assumed to be achieved by virtue of the formal language systems that one does or does not know.

Speaking on behalf of "diversity" or "students of color" raised particular issues for me because of the degree to which I recognized ignorances in my own experience and understanding about what it means to be discriminated against or stereotyped on the basis of one's ethnic identity. The danger is that I might, in the name of speaking for marginalized groups within the academy, actually perpetuate prejudices because of my own ignorances or, worse, that my speaking on behalf of "diversity" might lead others (white people) to falsely believe that by feeling comfortable with the Anglo-ness in me, they have pushed themselves to examine their own stereotypes and prejudices. These struggles were informed by how I saw privilege working in the context of hetero/homosexual identification. I came to understand something about the dangers of one's privileges and ignorances when claiming a marginalized identity because of experiences I had had as a lesbian. I came to know what it is like to have to endure another level of silencing and marginalization as a result of a heterosexually privileged other's self-serving and willfully ignorant assertions. The following example—an especially poignant experience—drove this point home for me.

During a graduate seminar on rhetorical theory and criticism, a white female peer and I were giving a presentation on feminist rhetorical criticism. As we began our presentation, my peer quickly proclaimed that she considered herself a lesbian, referring to Adrienne Rich's (1993) concept of "lesbian continuum" from an article that was on our reading list. She did not make this proclamation as a way of illustrating how Adrienne Rich develops her notion of a "lesbian continuum," how it is designed to bring to visibility and understanding about a human experience that has been systematically silenced, or how it is indebted to a long history of oppression endured by practicing lesbians. This peer was an openly married and practicing heterosexual. Her husband had been a regular visitor to the department, was part of our Sunday softball games, and showed up with his wife to all of our social gatherings. By simply declaring that she was a lesbian and then going on without identifying the range of the continuum and the differences encountered depending on where one is on that continuum, she erased the concrete experiences of struggle faced by sexually practicing lesbians. Everyone in that classroom knew both her and her

husband. In claiming an identity as a lesbian, she erased the particularities and risks that I faced as a someone who could not carry the heterosexual privilege she took for granted. Without contextualizing her claim
with an understanding of the differences between her identification as a
lesbian and sexually practicing lesbians, she sought to gain status by virtue of her "lesbian" connections to the women in her life. When I spoke
next, I alerted our audience to the difference between claiming an identification on the basis of being emotionally connected to women and actually living a life and engaging in practices that put one at risk within a
concrete social world. I saw my peer as seeking to benefit from the status
of "being a lesbian" without ever having engaged the emotionally difficult and socially threatening circumstance of being at risk because of her
lesbian identification.

I did not have a problem with her identifying herself as a lesbian as a
way to gain visibility for the importance of her relationships with women.
But her failure to identify the privileges and comforts of being a clearly
identifiable heterosexual in her daily life erased the concrete risks experienced by lesbians who cannot carry her heterosexual privilege. In this
case, her speaking "as a lesbian" benefited only herself in claiming a status unavailable to our mostly male—and, as far as I was aware, heterosexual—audience. The selfish ends of her discursive strategy were confirmed for me months later at a social gathering when she told me how
"angry" she was with me for "discrediting" her in front of our peers. Her
priorities were clearly aligned with the authority and power entailed within
the discourses of the graduate classroom. She stood willfully ignorant regarding the extent to which her utterances silenced and erased the experiences of those whose sexuality could not be lived so unselfconsciously
as her own. This experience, during a crucial period of my developing
ethnic identity, led me to consider very seriously the kinds of social discriminations that get perpetuated when someone like myself, a Mexican
American who can pass, speaks on behalf of or represents a marginalized
group such as Chicanas.[11] It also led me to think back, very carefully, about
my family life when I was growing up and the extent to which I lived with
traces of a Mexican American cultural heritage.

SEARCHING THROUGH MY FATHER'S BURIED PAST: IDENTIFYING THE KNOWING-UNKNOWN

There is a reason why I did not learn Spanish as I grew up, and it has
to do with my father's complex and mostly hidden life history. It has taken
me a long time to be able to write with empathy and understanding about
my father's life. I have, for many years, been very angry at my father—

angry mostly about his profound silences and the many distances they create. As I have struggled in my adult life to understand the circumstances of my own life when I was growing up, I have looked to my father's life as a place to build understanding. The details about my father's life that I provide here have come only very recently. Finally, long after I had begun writing about my ethnic identity and family history, I called my father on the telephone and said, "Can I ask you some questions?" I then moved through a formal interview protocol dealing with questions about the facts of his and his parents' life and about Spanish, education, religion, holiday celebrations, and experiences of discrimination. He seemed willing to respond and elaborate. He answered all my questions and even encouraged me to ask again. Yet I felt a strong twinge of anger at his encouragement because he was acting as if he was then and had always been open to sharing with me his experiences growing up.

Prior to that direct and formal interview, I had asked my father, on several occasions throughout my life, about his life while growing up—his father, his family, his experiences, and so on. I can never recall a time when he gave me anything more than a curt response. During my year (1990–1991) at the University of California at Santa Barbara, where I was a Chicana dissertation fellow, I saw my father and grandmother more regularly than I had since I was eleven years old. At that time he and my grandmother lived together in Simi Valley, California.[12] Emboldened in my effort to understand my cultural heritage, I asked my father what his father was like. He began telling me how his father was like my mother's father, and that was why he was always glad that we were so close to my mother's parents. On another occasion during that time, I was conversing with my father and grandmother when the issue of cultural identity and discrimination came up. My grandmother looked at me hard (yet kindly), pressed her lips tightly together, stiffened her back, and shook her head back forth. Her body was saying, "Yes, it was bad. Life was hard. We don't talk about those things." It was also during this conversation that my father told me that he was glad I was at UCSB and in the Chicano Studies Department because it meant that I could make a difference for others. Despite the many and different distances that have predominated in our relationship at various times, my father has always managed in subtle but powerful ways to communicate unequivocally that he supports me and believes in my choices even when he sees things very differently and would have made very different choices for himself.

Born in McAllen, Texas, in 1928, Octavio Martinez grew up very poor. When my father was very young, the family moved. First they moved to Brownsville, but a few years later they finally settled in Houston. Both his parents were bilingual, though his father had only a third-grade education and his mother an eighth-grade education. The family spoke Spanish inside the home and English outside the home. My father's father, Octavio Tergo Martinez, was a musically inclined common laborer who struggled to provide for his family. I never knew my grandfather. He died of a stroke in 1947, when my father was nineteen years old.

My father tells me that he saw blatant discrimination as he was growing up. As kids, he and his younger brother and sister could swim in the public swimming pool on Sunday evenings only—they cleaned the pool on Monday. Certain "Anglo only" barber shops were off limits to my father and his two siblings. But he also says that the social markers he noticed most were class markers. He says that for every Anglo kid who acted in discriminatory ways toward him, there were other Anglo kids who did not. At the same time he saw a certain disrespect for self and others carried out in the actions of some of the people around him. He says that he felt that there was more discrimination within the Mexican American community than from the Anglo community—a perception certainly encouraged by the internalized racism that functions within a racist culture.

It seems that at a young age my father identified a certain pettiness and ignorance among the poor "Mexican" people in his neighborhood. In this respect, my father has always had a sense of class. Not in the sense of having money but in the sense of having pride and consideration for oneself and others. In his professional life, my father has always been known as a demanding but fair executive. He supported the advancement of anyone who demonstrated the ability and commitment, without regard to race, ethnic heritage, marital status, or gender. Growing up in the world he did, he saw the Anglo world as one where he had a greater chance of being valued and rewarded for his work and abilities than he did in Mexican American communities, where the opportunities for social advancement were small. I get the feeling, from many years of listening to my father's brief and message-sending stories about his professional life, that he believes in equal opportunity but not affirmative action. He is very clear that *life is not fair.* It never has been, and it never will be. A staunch Republican, my father believes in the economic survival of the fittest. I am sure that he carries the memories of his own economically impoverished childhood very closely within him. I am sure that he suffered greatly during his childhood. On many occasions my father has said to me that he has achieved more in his life than he ever could have imagined, as if he could lose it all tomorrow and it would be okay.

After completing high school, my father enlisted in the Navy so that he could take advantage of the GI Bill and get a college education. When he finished his time in the Navy, he moved to southern California and entered the University of California at Los Angeles. It was in California that he met my mother, in church. When I asked my father about why he chose to marry an Anglo woman, he said that he did not decide to marry an Anglo woman; there was less discrimination against Mexican Americans out there. He felt that there was less discrimination against Mexican Americans in California and that the culture out there gave him more of a chance to be successful on his own merits. I think that my father wanted to be successful in the Anglo world, and marrying an Anglo woman just fit with those aspirations—not that any Anglo woman would do. But because he put himself where the opportunities were—in Anglo communities—it was more likely that he would come to marry an Anglo woman.[13] By the time he graduated from UCLA, he and my mother had had my older brother and sister. Education was, for him, entirely about the survival of his family. Both he and my mother worked full time as my father took a full load of classes. He knew that little piece of paper that said "bachelors degree" would open doors for him. A very intellectually curious man, my father has often said that he would have loved to study economics, but he did not have a choice. He knew that he needed a degree in business to make his way into the corporate world and thus move himself and his family up the socioeconomic scale.

My father's constant refrain to me and my brothers and sisters as we were growing up was "Go to school. Go to school. Go to school." He did not mean high school. I resisted his advice for a while. As I was growing up, I never felt connected to school or education. I was much more interested in being outside and taking in the southern California sunshine that felt like my birthright. I finally did take my father's advice, recognizing that if I wanted to do anything with my life, I needed a college education. It is ironic that education ended up giving me the space to seek out the opening of my own human horizons and thus also the means by which to look at things that he seemed so deliberately to keep away from me and my brothers and sisters.

When my father settled in California, he left his life (though not his connection to his family) behind in Texas. Because my father had grown up very poor, he had lived the pain, suffering, and injustices endured by the poor. Thinking as much as I have about my father's life and trying to understand it as deeply as I can, I get the feeling that growing up poor does something to you. "We were poor," my father says, "not 'economically deprived'; we were poor." There's a certain character and pride about my father. I think it comes from never forgetting where you come from, how hard your life was, and thus never taking for granted all the good things you have in your life. But, having accumulated all those good things—those comforts of middle-class success in the United States—the avenues that he had available to him for communicating to his children the painful realities of his own childhood become fewer. My father is an assimilationist: "I'm American," my father says emphatically, "not Mexican American, American." Yet I have recently begun to appreciate how—

despite his refusal to identify with his Mexican cultural heritage—deep his commitment to *la familia* has always been. Despite all the distances he seemed to create between us, his children, and his own childhood experiences as a "poor American of Mexican descent," I have finally come to see the ways in which he has always sought to provide for us the benefits of his understanding of human suffering and dignity. But it has taken me a long time to get here.

MAKING SENSE OF GROWING UP:
DESCRIBING THE UNKNOWING-KNOWING

There were various times during my childhood when I thought that my father's father was killed in the war. At other times I thought that he had died of a heart attack while digging ditches. There are still many things that I do not know about my father and his family. There have always been glaring silences surrounding my father that have stood impenetrable to me for as long as I have lived.

We were a family of five kids. My older sister and brother are seven and six years older than me, respectively. I am an identical twin and have a brother who is one year older than my twin and me. We lived in a seven-bedroom house with a three-car garage, two fireplaces, a wet bar, a swimming pool, and an outside fire pit. We moved to that house in 1965, when I was four years old. It was my father's position as an executive vice president for Teledyne that brought us to that neighborhood. As a young child I remember my parents throwing cocktail parties; we had a definitively white upper-middle-class lifestyle.

From the perspective of those Anglos encountering me in that middle-class white world of my childhood, my surname rarely signified anything other than Mexican American. I remember being a very little girl, dressed up in Sunday clothes, standing outside the church after services, adults talking. Then one adult leaned down to me, smiled broadly, and asked me if I spoke Spanish. At the time I was an expert in playing the cute little girl and responded by smiling shyly, twisting side to side on my feet, and uttering an elongated, "Noooo." Always, for as long as I can remember, the question, "Do you speak Spanish?" follows the Anglo-other's recognition of my surname. I think I knew then, standing outside that church, as I have known all my life, that Spanish will never be a language through which I will be able to communicate with my father. I do remember wondering why I did not learn Spanish as I was growing up. I knew that my father spoke it, but he never uttered a word in Spanish to my mother or us kids. I have, throughout my life, felt cheated in not having access to my father's Spanish language. But there was no way for a little girl to take up such a question with her father. I knew, even as an adult formally interviewing my father, that it was too dangerous to ask my father why he never spoke Spanish with us kids or why he did not at least speak Spanish with his mother when she visited us during my childhood. I heard my grandmother speak Spanish with her sister and my aunt. I knew that *mija* and *mijita* were Spanish words of endearment toward me. But my father's Spanishly silence sent powerful messages to me that to this day I do not fully comprehend. As a child I just learned to take the Anglos' question in stride, creating a full repertoire of responses to deal with any conversation that might ensue from such a question. I pushed the questions about speaking Spanish into the unknowing consciousness that dominated my childhood.

Yet there was a knowing to this unknowingness that also dominated my childhood. As a family, we ate tacos every Friday night; on those nights our dinner featured our Mexican cookware and serving dishes. I was a proficient taco maker before I was a teenager. I knew that we had some special connection to the Mayan calendar on our living room wall. We lived in that house until my parents got a divorce in 1978. Six years earlier, in 1972, my father had moved out of the house and back to Texas to start up a new business with his cousin. Despite the fact that my father moved out of the house when I was eleven years old, there was some deep emotional way in which I *never* felt abandoned by him. As a young corporate executive, my father had spent a lot of time traveling. There was something about his very quiet and determined way that communicated a lot to me regardless of his lengthy absences. As I have gotten older, I have, more than anything else, felt angry at knowing the deep humanity in this man yet having such time-limited access to it. When I was growing up, money and his role as provider were the dominant signs through which he communicated to me. As an adolescent and young adult, there were many times when I felt anger churning inside of me, and I wanted to yell at him, "Your credit card is not a substitute for you!" But as a child I think I was more angry at him for being gone so much when he did live at home than for being gone after he finally moved out of the house. I remember feeling a little guilty that I did not really miss him after he moved out.

As I have reflected on my life in an effort to make sense of the Mexican in me, I have come to focus on specific events connected to my father and through which I can point to ever so subtle traces of a heritage that was mostly hidden. My father never really shared anything about his life growing up with me. There were only a few occasions here and there when he would tell a story about his childhood, brief and to the point, always to illustrate to me and my brothers and sisters just how fortunate we were. The recurrent theme of my father's stories was one of living on the edges of survival, in poverty, ridiculed by other Mexicans who had more.

Because my brothers and sisters and I grew up in relative affluence, we never understood the value of having a new pair of shoes or a new jacket the way my father did. Somehow or another I think I had always gotten his message about human respect and dignity; my father has always taken it on himself to lecture his children about honesty, integrity, and respect. His own sense of ethics, respect, and determination were a big part of what made him so successful as a corporate executive, I am sure. There were huge gaps between the lives one can lead growing up poor versus relatively affluent. Growing up, I could not really understand these gaps, but I did have a general sense that there was something wrong with me for expecting that I would have what I needed. I realize now that when he grew up, he did not know that he would have what he needed. Only as an adult was it possible for me to understand how profoundly different my father's growing-up life and my own were. I can see very clearly how in my own growing-up world I could take many, many things for granted that my father never could have.

I always identified strongly with my father; perhaps his absences heightened that identification. I always listened to and watched him very carefully. His short and curt stories, combined with his profound silence about the whole of his life history, silenced my natural curiosities and left me feeling a deep and profound sense of something being hidden. My effort to understand my father's life experiences, in the face of his withholding those experiences, has been a crucial aspect of my own development of Chicana identity. This silence about the past and the feeling of something bad being hidden has, to a large degree, defined what limited ethnic heritage has carried forward through the assimilated lifestyle provided by my father's success in the dominant U.S. American culture.[14]

Because of my father's resilient silence, I feel a profound sense of betrayal in writing about experiences that are so private and personal. I also feel a sense of betrayal in working so hard to understand the Mexican cultural heritage that my father seemed so determined to deny. When I first began to reflect seriously about my father's cultural heritage, I felt a faint but clear sense that to search through my father's buried past was to risk encountering demons or evils of some sort. Over time, that sense of evils to be discovered has subsided and given way to a deeper understanding of the cultural and historical context in which my father—and many other Americans of Mexican descent—made the choice to assimilate in ways big and small. Reading the work of Chicana and Chicano scholars has been crucial in allowing me to see around my father's silences and understand his own place in history and thus the forces that led him to make the choices he did. I have come to the point now where I see my "betrayal" not as one of my father as much as of a racist culture that denies its own acts of oppression and continues to use Mexicans and Mexican Americans as scapegoats.

LOOKING TO THE HISTORY OF THE CHICANO PEOPLE: ENGAGING THE KNOWING-UNKNOWN

Identifying racist-assimilationist culture as the real object of my betrayal is possible only with the recognition that the unknowing-knowing that dominated my childhood was not peculiar to myself or my family's history—that it is the means and effect through which racist-assimilationist culture perpetuates itself. Coming to this realization required a certain span of time during which I had to live with and sort through the ambiguities entailed within the preknowing-knowing that first opened the door to my conscious engagement with questions about my racial and ethnic heritage. Once these questions attained a certain noematic status, it was possible for me to begin asking explicit questions about the history of the Chicano people, of the native people of this land, and of my relation to them. Being able to ask these questions explicitly, however, does not mean that the ambiguities of the preknowing-knowing go away. As I began asking questions explicitly, I retained much of the ambiguity of the preknowing-knowing and thus searched for "answers" that I felt were less ambiguous than others. For this reason, I entered into Chicano/a studies through the work of Chicana lesbians. I felt that I had some solid footing in understanding the experiences of other lesbians and realized that by following the paths undertaken by Chicana lesbians, I might be able to take up the experiences of Chicanos and Mexican Americans generally. Books like *Chicana Lesbians: The Girls Our Mothers Warned Us About* (Trujillo 1991) and *Compañeras: Latina Lesbians* (Ramos 1987) gave me a wide range of experiences and perspectives from which to make my own connections.

I have used Emma Pérez's essay "Gulf Dreams" (1991), for example, to connect the incredible passion we feel in our lesbian relationships and the social binds those passions bring for us to the passions and struggles we feel within the context of a racist culture. The feelings and struggles that fill the pages of Pérez's brave essay allowed me to connect with the experience of having to keep our most deep and powerful feelings hidden because of social restriction. The sexual attraction between her and another young women remains unspoken and gets sublimated as each pursues relationships with young men, some brown, some white. In the "play" of color, a young Chicana in school sees through the "conqueror's lies in history books" but remains mostly silent in surviving the Anglo teacher and her racist attempts to encourage the students to be glad that "Texas is in America" (Pérez 1991, 104). Reading the work of Chicana lesbians, I am reminded of the profound silences that capture our histories and keep them bound to the Anglo-racist accounts; they are silences that have also captured our lesbian passion.

In following along with the work of Chicana lesbians, I have been able to recognize the ways in which I have always felt connections to and curiosities about my Native American and mestizo heritage. But because of my father's own silences and our social circumstances, those connections and curiosities got sublimated as I moved through my everyday life of growing up. My father's deep humanity, it seems to me, has also developed through profound silences about his own suffering. Out of this suffering grew a great spirit and passion through which he set himself to the task of rising above that suffering and creating the circumstances so that his own family would never have to suffer the way he did. That my father's effort to achieve success and comfort for his family pushed him down a road of assimilation speaks volumes about the racist logic carried out in the legacy of colonialism. To understand the effort to assimilate simply as a betrayal to one's culture obscures the totality of circumstances in which Mexican Americans have—across generations and in a multitude of ways—struggled to survive.

By looking to the totality of circumstances in which Mexican Americans have struggled, I have been able to understand the ways in which all of us "darker others" have been objects of Euro-American ethnocentrism and its self-righteous domination (Acuña 1981). It is an insight that was first provoked for me by Martha Barrera's essay "Café con Leche" (1991). In this essay, Barrera addresses issues about being "ethnic enough" and whether "hanging around anglos" makes one's own ethnic heritage "corrupted." This essay helped me to feel connection to the varying degrees of struggle that all Mexican Americans face with regard to Anglo presence. Coming to see the commonality in the struggle with Anglo presence—both within our own psyches and as part of the very structure of social relations carried in our collective histories—provided a crucial point of connection for me. With such a point of connection, I have come to embrace the complex history of my family heritage—its mestizo roots from my father and the traces of Native American heritage from my mother's mostly Anglo side. In learning about these histories, I can come to terms with the confusing messages I got during my childhood and thus also with my own identity as a Chicana. In this way I am also able to move beyond the internal questions and make connections with other Chicanas, Chicanos, and people of color. With these connections it becomes possible to see generations of struggle and embrace a history that the colonizing logic of Euro-American culture would have erased.

In coming to make these connections, I am deeply indebted to the work of many Chicana scholars who have offered rereadings of history going back to the original colonization of this land of the Americas. Chicana scholars have been especially insistent on rereading what Norma Alarcón (1983) calls the "male mythology of *La Malinche.*" It is through the demythifying of La Malinche that Chicana scholars such as Alarcón (1983, 1990), Anzaldúa (1987), Mirandé and Enríquez (1979), Moraga (1983), and Pérez (1991) have forced a reconsideration of the "loyalist versus betrayer" binarism, especially as it is tied to Chicanas' sexuality, an issue I foreground in the following chapter. Coming to learn about the legacy of colonialism and its effects on generations of mestizo people has given me important connections to men of color. When Ana Castillo (1994) critiques the Anglo use of "machismo" by citing the Anglo's own masculine bravado inherent in their attitudes of conquest, she is exposing how the mythmaking of the dominant culture serves their hegemonic interests. In learning about the history of the southwestern United States from the perspective of Chicanas/os and considering it in the context of my father's life choices, I have come to understand something of how traces of history live in the present, how they function preconsciously and unknowingly, much in the same way that my assimilated family life still carries traces of my Mexican cultural heritage. Or, to put it another way, I have come to see how my own being-in-communication-with the anonymity of history and culture carries forward the legacy of racist practices into my own taken-for-granted self-understanding. It seems crucially important that we engage in a cultural recovery that directly counters the racist legacy of colonialism that continues to encourage assimilation of all sorts. It has been through the courageous writing by Chicana lesbians that I have been able to enter into a consideration of the very life circumstances by which I have carried my own mestizo ancestry and thus recover a heritage that would have otherwise been lost.

Having engaged a series of personal reflections and theoretical arguments in an effort to interrogate the very modes of consciousness through which I have come to consciousness as a Chicana, it is necessary to shift focus toward the cultural body and the cross-generational struggles fought on it. This shift to an interrogation of the cultural body is important for several reasons. Although the interrogation of personal experiences is an essential and necessary terrain through which a critical phenomenology of race or ethnicity must travel, such an interrogation is insufficient in and of itself. It is always possible that in our own private reflection we deceive ourselves. Even if we are not self-deceptive, it is difficult to adequately sort through and separate the idiosyncrasies of one person's experience from those experiences that are bound directly to the social and cultural momentum in which we are located. Interrogating cross-generational silences and struggles can allow us to see the ways in which particular experiences are engendered by a racist-sexist-heterosexist culture. In this way it might be possible to identify how transformations occurring in the present time are made possible by struggles engaged in preceding generations.

My effort in the next chapter is to interrogate the conditions of the cultural and historical body from which the personal experiences described in this chapter are necessarily related. The cultural body, in my consideration of it below, necessarily focuses on ambiguity and changing conceptions of self and social worlds across generations. The ambiguities I encountered in my personal experience are linked semiotically with the conceptions of race and ethnicity developed over centuries on the Central/North American continent—conceptions of race that are essentially racist and that serve the interests of the dominating Euro-centric U.S. American culture. My effort will be to trace through the history of resistances against these dominating forces as radically and ambiguously embodied by contemporary Chicana lesbians. In taking up this effort, I challenge typical binary-based conceptions of loyalty versus betrayal as it pertains to mestizas. In so doing, I will be establishing what I hope is a more textured terrain from which we understand and interrogate the relationship between assimilation, survival, and the racist cultural terms in which struggles of life are waged.

NOTES

1. There is some question as to whether Mexican Americans constitute a "race" and are therefore "racialized." While certain Mexican Americans are more easily racially marked because of skin color, speech patterns, and communities of residence, it is also true than many Mexican Americans have very few of these racial markings and are therefore much less likely to be racialized within the general momentum of cultural signification. It might make more sense, then, to talk about the degree of ethnicity carried forward by Mexican Americans. Despite these differences, I retain "racialization" to emphasize the degree to which racism functions as an exclusion. Racist exclusions are deployed variously throughout a culture, and some people will, by virtue of the obvious signs of race, be more subjected by those racist exclusions. While it is important to not conflate the wide range of degrees to which different people and groups are objects of racist exclusion, the racialized knowledge that makes racist exclusion possible is equally present given the fact that we live in a racist culture. Gordon's work on antiblack racism (1995) makes this same point. See also Goldberg (1993, 74–78).

2. I am using the phenomenological terms *noesis* and *noema* here. However, I could equally well use the language of semiotics, of the interpretant as it enables the meaning derived. See Lanigan (1988) for informed discussions of the semiotic emphasis in the work of Merleau-Ponty. See also Merrell (1995).

3. I take this concept of an "unknowing-knowing" from Eve Kosofsky Sedgwick (1990), although I have changed the second term in my usage. As Sedgwick describes a feature of coming out, "It can bring about the revelation of a powerful unknowing *as* unknowing, not as a vacuum or as the blank it can pretend to be but as a weighty and occupied and consequential epistemological space" (77).

4. It is supremely ironic to me that I attended California State University, Northridge, as I began broaching questions regarding my Mexican American ancestry. That university must be recognized for its leading role in the development and sustenance of Chicana and Chicano studies as a legitimate and important academic discipline. The Chicano Studies and Pan African Studies Departments were established in 1969 after protests by Chicano and African American students that included the taking over of the administration building, the holding of hostages, and a presentation of demands (Muñoz 1989). I remember visiting the department at CSUN, talking with one of the professors and several students. I remember being struck by the beautiful murals, the fliers, and other signs of activism spread about. I realize that I was so much at the beginning of coming to recognize the significance of the Chicano struggle for my own life and history that I could not really begin to take up and engage what that department offered me.

5. I must emphasize again the dynamic interrelation between and among the three modes of consciousness I am outlining here. Although I use the past tense to indicate that there were precise moments in my life in which I can identify the emergence of each mode of consciousness, the modes themselves remain in constant interaction. My movement through and about them necessarily continues.

6. My focus on "modes of consciousness" is informed by and deeply indebted to Richard L. Lanigan (1988) and his work on the phenomenology of communication and to Chela Sandoval (1991) and her work on the theory and method of oppositional consciousness in a postmodern world.

7. In using the word *world* in the subhead "Entering a Chicana Lesbian World," I have in mind the notion of "'World'-Traveling" developed by María Lugones (1987) in what is a truly remarkable essay.

8. My Ph.D. course work focused heavily on existential and semiotic phenomenology, particularly the work of Maurice Merleau-Ponty, Michel Foucault, and semiotics in the European (Saussure, Hjemsleve, Jakobson, Barthes, and Eco) and American (Reusch, Bateson, and Peirce) traditions. Because I was in a speech communication department, I was encouraged to take the concreteness of my own daily living communicative experience very seriously. There was a clearly existential feature emphasized by our graduate director, Thomas J. Pace. I am deeply indebted to Tom for creating a graduate program in which we were encouraged to take up the struggles of our own particular human existences. My sense is that too few graduate programs actually do this.

9. This is one reason why it is so important to have more people of color in graduate programs. My own conversations with Norman Greer and Shirlene Holmes, fellow graduate students and African Americans in my department, allowed me and other graduate students to take up issues of racism more directly. Were it not for Norman's and Shirlene's presence, it would have been harder for me to take up such questions as directly.

10. My use of "Spanishly" is taken from Merleau-Ponty's use of the word "languagely." He writes, "There is a 'languagely' ['langagière'] meaning of language which effects the mediation between my as yet unspeaking intention and words, and in such a way that my spoken words surprise me myself and teach me my thought" (1964, 88). See also Merleau-Ponty (1986).

11. It was an essay by Linda Alcoff (1992) that gave me important insight into understanding my own struggle with my privileged background. Alcoff's essay provided a crucial foundation from which I was able to successfully work through the very confusing set of circumstances that I had to negotiate in order to come to speak as a Chicana.

12. Symbolisms reverberate for me in the fact that my father used to live in Simi Valley, across the street from the Ronald W. Reagan Presidential Library and Museum. Simi Valley is where the Rodney King criminal trial was held. The Simi Valley jury found the police officers who beat King not guilty, sparking rebellions all over Los Angeles.

13. I am a little troubled here by referring to my mother, Patricia C. Martinez, as some anonymous "Anglo" woman. Who I am today is as much a consequence of my mother's life and history as it is my father's. The reason why I focus on my father presently is because my questions about my ethnic and racial history all seemed to direct from him and his life. The Native American ancestry that I recognized as coming from my mother's side of the family is so much more ethereal and intertwined with the Anglo aspects of her history that it seems to fall out as I sift through the experiences available for me to grasp and work with.

14. Cristina González, in a very important conversation, helped me to understand this point; in her own work with Native American people, she has identified some ways in which the desecration of their cultures, blatantly exacted by the forces of Anglo racism, has resulted in the carrying forward of dysfunctions as cultural heritage.

3

RADICAL AMBIGUITIES AND THE CHICANA LESBIAN: BODY TOPOGRAPHIES ON CONTESTED LANDS

The history of Americans of Mexican descent living in the southwestern United States is complex, diverse, and uneasily characterizable. Spanning a history that traces back nearly five hundred years to precolonial time, this land and the people born on it can be said to have always been living in a state of warring struggle. Yet the content and expression of this state of struggle—much like the people themselves—exists in multiple forms and to varying degrees. While events like the Mexican Revolution are markers for the people whose histories lie on this land, there are other, less historically tangible and thus differently important markers signifying conditions of battle against an oppressor. They are markers that tell us a great deal about human struggle, human liberation, and human transformation.

In the preceding chapters I have emphasized the way in which ambiguity suffuses our human existence by virtue of our rootedness in a lived body as it is inextricably bound to and in-communication-with the social, historical, and cultural world. This ambiguity that suffuses our human existence can be understood in at least two distinct and related ways: at the level of the social and cultural momentum present at a given moment in time and space and at the level of the person who is inextricably in-communication-with that social and cultural momentum. Ambiguity at the first level accounts for the fact that no matter how total or fully encompassing a dominate discourse is—for example, the dominant racializing discourse of contemporary U.S. American culture in which persons are assumed to naturally fit or not to fit into discrete racial designations—there will always be those who defy the normative categories, who challenge our ordinary perception, and who thus help bring to light the very functioning of that dominant discourse itself. Ambiguity at the second level accounts for the fact that persons who are situated in the same or very similar objective social conditions will often come to identify themselves, ascribe meaning to their experience, and hold aspirations for their future in radically different ways. When we have conditions of ambiguity that suffuse both these levels, we have greater potentiality for a *radical ambiguity* whereby the very terms and conditions making it possible for one to say what was said, think what was thought, feel what was felt, and do what was done may come into fuller view. On interrogating these terms and conditions, we have the potentiality of stepping out from under the ordinary binary and taxonomic distinctions that give social, historical, and cultural forces their normative thrust.

In this chapter I would like to focus on the Chicana lesbian[1] as occupying a place of radical ambiguity that, when read through a history of the land of the southwestern United States, problematizes the "assimilationist versus nationalist" and "complicitous-traitor versus loyal-culturalist" binarisms. Indeed, the reading offered here intends to suggest how the emergence of the Chicana lesbian as a site of struggle demands a reconsideration of these binarisms; such a reading simultaneously creates different possibilities for understanding and achieving radical transformation for both the person and the social world.

The construction of the Chicana lesbian, her situation as a radically ambiguous situation, and her location within the heterogeneous forces of the dominant social momentum (white, European, colonial, heterosexual, and capitalist) is intricately intertwined with the histories, cultures, and lands from which her possibility emerges. Given such a locatedness, the possibility of the Chicana lesbian emerges as a struggle that is located *within as it fights against* the multifarious deployment of colonial oppression and racist assimilation. Within the meaningfulness of the life-world struggle of the Chicana lesbian, we have a site of communicative production whose interrogation suggests how radical transformations might obtain in the concrete practices of the academic-activist—a site of practice that can effectively serve the academy's own perpetuation of various forms of oppression and dominance. This is a point emphasized by bell hooks (1990) when she says,

> It is sadly ironic that the contemporary discourse [postmodernism] which talks the most about heterogeneity, the decentered subject, declaring breakthroughs that allow recognition of Otherness, still directs its critical voice primarily to a specialized audience that shares a common language rooted in the very master narratives it claims to challenge. . . . Without adequate concrete knowledge of and contact with the non-white "Other," white theorists may move in discursive theoretical directions that are threatening and potentially disruptive of that critical practice which would support radical liberation struggle. (25–26)

Given my primary concern with the site of practice, or *location*, as an essential factor in the content and expression of the radical ambiguity characterizing the Chicana lesbian, it is important to emphasize three in-terrelated points that turn the focus back on the location and situation of the production of this academic work itself. First, the emergence of the Chicana lesbian as a self-declared identity is directly and necessarily linked to activism, intellectualism, and artistry of all kinds both inside and out-side the academy. Chicano studies, for example, has never existed except as activist—the hegemony of the "American melting pot" creates a social momentum that literally prohibits (excludes) its existence. The coercive bleaching effect of the "melting pot" makes difference unrecognizable and reinforces the normative goodness of whiteness and badness of darkness. Thus, we have the notion of a "successful Mexican American" as one who embodies all the signifiers of white middle-class heterosexual American—one who can be understood entirely within the "American" ideology and thus poses no threat to the white-dominance structure that is America. Within this racist-assimilationist context, declaring oneself Chicano and taking up the study of the Chicano people is never just an academic en-deavor but always already activist. Even a cursory look at the people and locations producing the Chicana lesbian as a site of resistance suggests that the boundary between inside and outside the academy, between activism, intellectualism, and artistry, is virtually unintelligible. As Cherríe Moraga (1993) says about her own work, "So these are not essays as much as they are poems and these are not poems so much as they are essays. Possibly the distinction no longer matters—between the poem and the essay, be-tween my art and my activism" (4).

Second, as a site of activism and resistance, the possibility of the Chicana lesbian as a self-adopted label shares important points of common-ality with other identities and communities produced in resistance to the domination of colonizing forces (e.g., African Americans, Asian Americans, and Native Americans).[2] Chela Sandoval (1991) makes this point when she argues for a specific form of consciousness (a "differential" conscious-ness) common to "U.S. third world women" precisely because of their similar histories of oppression and the hegemony of feminist theory:

> Both in spite of and yet because they represent varying internally colo-nized communities, U.S. third world feminists have generated a common speech, a theoretical structure which, however, remained outside the purview of the dominant feminist theory emerging in the 1970s, func-tioning within it—but only as the unimaginable. (1)

These points of commonality provide a basis on which the hegemony of colonization, even in a "post"-colonial time and within the colonizing state, can be recognized for the implicit logic that governs the practices of domi-nant (first world) states and comes to presence in the hearts and minds of generations of the Others who are the targets of colonial powers.[3] Indeed, these commonalties across various communities have been crucial components of the best theorizing within feminist academic practice over the past fifteen years.

While these points of commonality across Othered communities help expose the perversity and legacy of colonial domination, an important caution also needs to be raised. The similar situations of various groups of people relative to the dominating force colonialism/postcolonialism does not prevent the differences among and within these groups from themselves effecting the same logic of domination embodied by colonizers. Indeed, "divide and conquer" is alive and well as a strategy exacted by hegemonic forces precisely so as to continue domination.[4] Even a brief description of the situation of the Chicana lesbian illustrates this point: suspect in and suspecting of the European-American context, suspect in and suspecting of feminists, suspect in and suspecting of the Chicano community and even within *la familia,* the Chicana lesbian has no clear direction in which she might fully resist the heterogeneous forces of oppression she faces. The Chicana lesbian finds forces of sexist and heterosexist oppression working against her even in the midst of alliances built in the name of resistance against oppression. The experience of the Chicana lesbian thus situated suggests that activism and intellectualism that portends to radically subvert the conditions of domination must necessarily interrogate the condition and effects of its own practices within and across the various sites of its own possibility.

My third point, then, has to do exactly with the inseparability of the intellectual and activist from the concrete conditions in which she practices her intellectualism and activism, the inseparability of the (Chicana lesbian) theorist herself from that which she theorizes. An understanding of the situation of the Chicana lesbian as theorist, intellectual-activist, and academic demonstrates the imperative of a consciously engaged self-locatedness in one's practices where one takes an accountability for the effects of that locatedness and thus engages in a self-reflexive critical and analytic methodology (a semiotic and existential phenomenology) that allows for an interrogation of the conditions of production in the midst of its production—an interrogation of our very being-in-communication-with that is our intersubjective subjectivity.[5] This is a requirement also articulated by Butler (1993) when she suggests that "it is important to resist that theoretical gesture of pathos in which exclusions are simply affirmed as sad necessities of signification" (53).

In taking the positionality of the Chicana lesbian as subject matter, I intend to suggest how particular past historical presences construct her as an exclusion and thus as a potential site of radical transformation. This effort is much akin to Spivak's (1988) description of the subaltern studies group:

It can be advanced that their work presupposes that the entire socius, at least in so far as it is the object of their study, is what Nietzsche would call a *fortgesetzte Zeichenkette*—a "continuous sign-chain." The possibility of action lies in the dynamics of the disruption of this object, the breaking and relinking of the chain. This line of argument does not set consciousness over against the socius, but sees it as itself also constituted as and on a semiotic chain. It is thus an instrument of study which participates in the nature of the object of study. (198)

As a multiply marginalized figure, the Chicana lesbian's exclusion is part and parcel of the dominant American-cultural meaning system (a continuous sign-chain) that makes her unintelligible. It is also, ironically, that very status as exclusion that offers the possibility of breaking that meaning system and bringing her to presence today. Describing the sites that produce her as an unintelligible by exclusion, however, also creates (is dependent on) other exclusions. Those exclusions must also be engaged precisely because they create the circumstances for the realization of new possibilities even while they close off still other possibilities.

One should not conclude, however, that all exclusions are created equally. The racist assimilation that characterizes U.S. American culture produces whiteness as norm and blackness (nonwhiteness) as different from (less than) that norm and operates with a level of force and dominance that simply cannot be paralleled to or equated with the productions of exclusions that happen *within* the exclusions produced by the deployment of racism and heterosexism that is the dominant U.S. American culture. A specification of the locations (and the presence of historical pasts) from which identities and practices are produced should highlight these differences as well. A similar point is made by Butler (1993) when she says,

Even if every discursive formation is produced through an exclusion, that is not to claim that all exclusions are equivalent: what is needed is a way to assess politically how the production of cultural unintelligibility is mobilized variably to regulate a political field, i.e., who will count as a "'subject,'" who will be required not to count. (207)

My effort here is to focus on the situation of consciousness when a subject is unintelligible (Chicana lesbian) and suggest how this situation offers the possibilities of radical transformation.

THE EMERGENCE OF "THE CHICANA LESBIAN"

The Chicana lesbian is, in one sense, a relatively recent phenomenon when one considers the nearly 500-year history of European domination in what is today Mexico and the southwestern United States. It has only been since the 1960s that "Chicano" as an identity designator has existed at all. The contemporary construction of "lesbian" (or "homosexual") is, likewise, quite specific to the latter half of this century (Foucault 1980; Faderman 1981). Though common knowledge today suggests that sexual relationships among people of the same sex have existed in all times and across all cultures, the cultural meanings ascribed to such behavior vary widely (Blackwood 1984). Considered in this way, the Chicana lesbian appears as a creation of this time, occurring in a synchronicity of the late twentieth-century United States.

Yet, in another sense, the construction of the Chicana lesbian represents the very struggle of the native peoples of North America against the heterogeneous forces of oppression sustained in the very history of this contested land—a history that bears directly on the meaningfulness of the life-world struggle for the self-declared Chicana lesbian today. The adoption of "Chicano" as an identity designator is directly linked to the long history of struggle of native and nonwhite (mestizo) people who have been the objects of Spanish and American-European colonization. Its adoption signifies a consciously engaged *resistance*. When "lesbian" is adopted in conjunction with "Chicana," we have a construction doubly laden with consciously engaged resistance that is posed *against itself from within*.

Such a double engagement problematizes the normative conditions of both the "nationalist" Chicano movement for its heterosexism and machismo and feminist academic theory and practice for its racism and hegemony (Broyles 1990; Yarbro-Bejarano 1990; Sandoval 1991). Even in the most obvious sense, the Chicana lesbian functions as an exclusion across three sites: within the Chicano movement, within the women's movement (and feminist academic practice), and within the dominant American culture.[6] Yet, in a much more subtle sense, the Chicana lesbian embodies a radical ambiguity that demonstrates the insufficiency of these more obvious sites as a basis for the Chicana lesbian to come to have knowledge (*savoir*) of herself—a knowledge of self ontologically contingent, existing in a state of radical ambiguity. In this way I am *not* engaged in a project to find the "true" site where the Chicana lesbian comes to "know herself." Rather, I am attempting to demonstrate that it is the insufficiency of these obvious sites that *is* the production of the Chicana lesbian. Thus, "self-knowledge" is not posited as achievable in the colloquial sense of knowing oneself but as a consciously engaged situation in which one's knowledge of what there is to know of the self and social world always exceeds one's ability to fully know (a knowing-unknown). It is this more subtle sense of consciousness of self and world that is therefore my primary focus in this chapter.

In the sections that follow, I begin with "Situating the Past," that is, with considering the presence of historical pasts in the production of the contemporary Chicana lesbian. I use the work of contemporary Chicanas and Chicana lesbians to inform the selection of key figures and events on the contested lands of the mestizo people in order to suggest how situations of radical ambiguity can create conditions for radical transformation. My effort is to suggest a certain carrying over of struggle, survival, and transformation carried across generations who have lived on these contested lands. These contested lands thus become more than merely soil on which we have set our feet but also constitute the very terrain of conscious experience that links people together across generational time and space. I then move to a "Self-Reflexive Interrogation" of the production of the discourse engaged in this academic work so as to engage the concrete reality present its production. This self-reflexive turn necessarily emphasizes contingency. I use *"contingency"* in the sense offered by Merleau-Ponty's (1964) "logic in contingency—an oriented system which nevertheless always elaborates random factors, taking what was fortuitous up again into a meaningful whole—an incarnate logic" (88). The effort here is to disclose the functioning of *difference* in the construction of the Chicana lesbian. This discussion leads me to consider the "Theoretical and Methodological Implications" of engaging the marginalized and excluded. Here I attempt to articulate how an activism and intellectualism produced from the location of the Chicana lesbian might interrogate the conditions of its own practice within and across its various sites so as to radically subvert conditions of domination in an exertion of existential freedom.

SITUATING THE PAST: THE MOTHER OF THE MESTIZO PEOPLE AND MESTIZO BORDERLANDS

In situating the historical past presences that produce the Chicana lesbian, we abandon the notion of an "original" people or situation that existed prior to oppression and to which we might seek to return. In this way we also abandon the notion of an "originating experience" that founds a subject that we call "Chicana lesbian" (Foucault 1972a, 215–237). Rather, we are looking to the past to see how it lives in consciousness and the concrete practices of this moment. Recognizing that "discourse cannot restore the totality of its history within a strict framework," we set ourselves about the task of "replacing . . . the theme of becoming . . . by the analysis of the *transformations* in their specifics" (Foucault 1972b, 227, 230).

The land of what is today the southwestern United States bears on it a nearly 500-year history of struggle against European colonization and its relentless and violent encroachments. The conquest of the Aztecs by Hernán Cortés in 1521 resulted in the near annihilation of the native peoples and initiated a proliferation of geographical and psychical "borderlands" that continues to this day:

> Before the Conquest, there were twenty-five million Indian people in Mexico and the Yucatán. Immediately after the Conquest, the Indian population had been reduced to under seven million. By 1650, only one-and-a-half-million pure-blooded Indians remained. The *mestizos*... founded a new hybrid race and inherited Central and South America. . . . Chicanos, Mexican-Americans, are the offspring of those first matings. (Anzaldúa 1987, 5)

These "borderlands" are first and foremost boundaries that serve the interests of the colonizing forces but that also function to exacerbate sexism and heterosexism within what has become the Chicano/Mexican American culture. In serving colonial interests, these borderlands have often divided the native peoples by setting up conditions for competing interests among themselves (particularly between women and men) and with other groups. In orchestrating this transcultural domination, the forces of colonial powers, in the actual deployment of that power, situate different groups as *mediums* for that power. There is some sense in which simply being an object of colonialism entails a carrying through of that power and its interests. In the context I am describing here, the colonized people become mediums of colonial power and thus assist in its deployment. This creates fractures *within* a previously self-identified group as some but not all persons within the group recognize the ways in which the group as construed by the dominant culture serves colonialist-racist interests. The same dynamics occur *between* previously identified groups who both become objects of colonial power.[7]

There is perhaps no figure that more strongly represents this colonial-driven division than Malintzin Tenepal, also know as La Malinche.[8] La Malinche, the person and the myth, epitomizes the conflicting interests orchestrated by the forces of colonization that, not surprisingly, use women's sexuality for the construction of a *male* mythology that retains presence in the many generations of mestizas and mestizos since the conquest. It is a mythology that, according to Cherríe Moraga (1983), is "carved into the very bone of Mexican/Chicano collective psychology" (176). La Malinche's impact on Chicanas is stark: "The persuasiveness of the myth is unfathomable, often permeating and suffusing our very being without conscious awareness" (Alarcón 1983, 184).

As the interpreter, guide, and mistress for Cortés, La Malinche is commonly understood to have facilitated the conquest. For that, she is considered both the "mother of the Mexican people" (the mestizos) and "La Chingada" (the fucked one), a traitor to her people. As a myth, La Malinche exists precisely because of what she is taken to represent for women's sexuality. As Norma Alarcón (1983) describes it,

> The male myth of Malintzin is made to see betrayal first of all in her very sexuality, which makes it nearly impossible at any given moment to go beyond the vagina as the supreme site of evil until proven innocent by way of virginity or virtue, the most pawnable commodities around. (183)

The omnipresence of the male myth of La Malinche creates a double bind for mestizas. One strategy for survival under the force of the myth is to demonstrate obedience and devotion to men. The privileging of male perspectives, male desires, and male children all reflect the logic of the myth of La Malinche. To enact this strategy is for Chicanas to embrace a status as inherently unreliable (sexually) and in need of proving differently. It is, as Alarcón puts it, a circumstance in which one eventually comes to self-hate.

A second strategy is to assert one's existential freedom and refuse to make one's life meaningful according to the male myth of La Malinche. Yet the persuasiveness of the myth within a conquered culture means that even in the assertion of one's existence in a "radical questioning" of the meaning system informing the social world, the Chicana/Chicana lesbian is taken as disobedient, nondevout, a traitor to her people (Alarcón 1983, 186). Alliances between Chicana lesbians and Chicanos that might otherwise be built to fight a common enemy in the colonizing forces are deeply and preconsciously encumbered from the beginning. For the self-declared Chicana lesbian (and Chicanas generally), the myth of La Malinche functions as a barrier to alliances that would allow her to *both* pursue her existential freedom and form alliances with her Chicano brothers against the forces of colonialism and racist assimilation.

The presence of the male myth of La Malinche constitutes a set up from the beginning. Recognizing this double bind of social circumstance, Chicanas and Chicana lesbian writers demonstrate a "pervasive preoccupation and influence of the myth" and the "need to demythify" it (Alarcón 1983, 187). It is through just this kind of work, which so deeply challenges bedrock notions structuring the meaning systems of Chicano/Mexican (and U.S. American) culture, that Chicana lesbians embody a radical ambiguity that contains the potentiality of radical transformation.

The terrain traveled in such radical transformation is, however, neither smooth nor imminently apparent. It occurs as a struggle within consciousness itself. Many Chicana lesbians today struggle across a variety of discursive contexts (as activists, academics, feminists, and artists) out of necessity and precisely because of the social double binds in which we find ourselves. As women, both heterosexual and lesbian, Chicanas are subjected by the male myth of La Malinche; both seek to recover and demythify her in their work in their activism, art, and intellectualism (González 2000). Such an effort bears some connection to feminist struggle. Yet to declare oneself feminist is also equated with disloyalty and thus acts of betrayal. The presence of the myth of La Malinche sets up circumstances in which coming to one's awareness of her lesbianism is prohibited; to openly declare oneself lesbian risks rejection of the most extreme sort. The effort to demythify La Malinche is an effort to create space where women can assert their own sexuality without stigmatization.

Having identified a mythological presence that is a key semiotic linkage in the meaning system of the Chicano/Mexican culture since the sixteenth-century conquest, I would like to turn briefly to a set of circumstances present for the people of the southwestern United States during the "postcolonial" period. My effort is to suggest that the double bind out of which the previously discussed Chicana writers seek to travel has certain circumstances that resonate with the experiences of the people of the Southwest during the "postcolonial" time. From this brief discussion, I will return to the work of one contemporary Chicana lesbian and again identify what I see as common circumstances in all of the situations I discuss.

HISTORICAL PAST PRESENCES AND THE CONTEMPORARY CHICANA LESBIAN

While it is clear that the mythical presence of La Malinche plays an important role in the Chicana lesbian's coming to a consciously engaged resistance to oppression, there are many other circumstances that demonstrate how colonization creates divisions that serve the interests of the colonizers. A brief discussion of the colonial-created divisions also illustrates the workings of various forms of resistance that defy the "assimilationist versus nationalist" and "complicitous-traitor versus loyal-culturalist" binarisms. I refer specifically to the northward expansion by the Spanish, the early nineteenth-century Mexican independence, and the 1848 Treaty of Guadalupe Hidalgo.

In their constant zeal for expansion, the Spanish-governed colonists of the late sixteenth and early seventeenth centuries forced their way northward and continued their effort to dominate other peoples native to those lands of what is today the southwestern United States. The colonizing relationships proliferated along with new generations of mixed-blood people situated within competing sets of interests (i.e., in a negatively ambiguous way[9]) orchestrated by the forces of colonization. This geographical expansion multiplies the psychical divisions among the various peoples subjected under colonization and creates layers on layers of often conflicting identifications. Yet, even for Mexican/mestizo settlers who did not apprehend themselves to be working at conflicting interests, the forces of colonization still bore down on their lives as the very conditions within which they etched out survival.

Between 1810 and 1825, Mexico freed itself from Spanish domination. In the northern frontier, the immediate effect of the fall of Spanish rule "was a laxity of control, as well as neglect, by Mexico" (Rebolledo and Rivero 1983, 7). The new Spanish and mestizo settlers faced complex circumstances of association with other people. Some Native Americans had been bought and sold as slaves and remained under control of the Spanish-Mexican settlers after the ending of Spanish rule. But the absence of force that came with the vacated presidios and military outposts left the mestizo settlers open targets for depredations by Native American tribes who were *reacting* "to the pressures from Anglos pushing West," taking away their native hunting grounds and lands, and generally threatening their very means of survival (Rebolledo and Rivero 1993, 7). Mestizo and Native Americans became enemies, fighting against each other for their very survival by virtue of colonial expansion from both the south and the east. The land of the southwestern United States becomes the field on which these colonial-orchestrated conflicting interests get played out long after the departure of formal Spanish rule.

The Treaty of Guadalupe Hidalgo in 1848—a U.S. American takeover of the land of what is now the southwestern United States—added another layer of psychical and geographical conflict for the people living on this land. The treaty formally allowed Mexican citizens living in this territory to become American citizens with all the accompanying rights. But in reality, Mexicanos (mestizos) were marked against the Euro-American migrant, their ways of living and speaking taken as inferior; "society became two-tiered, and racial and religious prejudice were evident" (Rebolledo and Rivero 1983, 9). Indeed, "racial slurs and derogatory comments about Mexicans appeared regularly in the *Congressional Record,* in newspapers, and . . . in travel accounts" (González 1993, 81).

"Belonging" to the United States, this land becomes a magnet for Euro-American migrants. The racism and socioeconomic pressures exacted with the westward expansion by Euro-Americans created circumstances where people of differently mixed blood simply knew that *how* they were identified ethnically made a difference (González 1993, 81). Mexicanos were positioned to identify with the logic of racism as they pursued simple survival. The robbing of native lands and the destruction of established ways of life left native peoples and Mexicanos in the position of having to employ capitalism ...ఎ a means of survival. The moment these already established communities engage in capitalist systems, they become entwined in the racism that informs the righteousness of white domination, a consequence that began developing well before the '848 Treaty of Guadalupe Hidalgo. Within the context of pervasive ethnic discrimination governed by the socioeconomic and cultural do   ation of white Euro-Americans, the Mexicanos developed specific patterns of survival in which they participated while struggling against the forces of Euro-American expansion (González 1993). The life of Doña Gertrudis Barceló, subject of the legend of "La Tules," illustrates this point well.

A prominent figure in the town of Santa Fe from the early 1800s until her death in 1852, Barceló was one of the town's most wealthy and well-respected citizens. She was revered in her community because of her continuous and generous support for others. She was a major figure and leader in a town that prospered despite difficult circumstances. There was, however, a double-edged sword to her success: While it helped create a vibrant and healthy community, it also created a place for Euro-American newcomers to become socialized and thus facilitated their eventual dominance (González 1993). In this way, Barceló gave "herself to the conquest, but not to the conquerors" (González 1993, 80).

The parallel to Malintzin Tenepal seems all too obvious: woman facilitating conquest of her own people. But in writing about La Tules, González—like Alarcón, Anzaldúa, Moraga, Rebolledo and Rivero, and many other Chicana writers (activists, artists, and academics-intellectuals)—demands a rethinking of mestizas in the (never having ceased) conquest. Consider, for example, the stark contrast between Barceló in Santa Fe and Padre Antonio José Martín   n the sister city of Taos. Unlike Santa Fe, which was gene ....y welcoming of newcomers, in Taos residents had killed newcomers. Padre Antonio José Martínez was "the famed resister to American encroachment . . . [who] opposed (in his separatist plar   nd principles) all that Barceló exemplified" (González 1993, 86). What sense do we make of these differences between Barceló and Martínez? Complicitor versus loyalist? What kind of "war" /as each engaged in? What values are we to assign to each strategy? How does gender and sexuality play into the values that we might come to assign to these different strategies? Would a revolution led by Martínez have done anything to challenge machismo or the taboos surrounding women's sexuality? The contrast between these two figures considered in the context of colonial expansion compels the recognition that the "complicitous-traitor versus loyal-culturalist" binarism is insufficient for understanding the war of consciousness engaged by the mestizo people of the southwestern United States.

As a marginal figure, Barceló's "life and legend contradict orthodox notions of marginality in a situation of conquest" (González 1993, 79). Her very (and extraordinary) success as a businesswoman in fact gave her the economic achievement that allowed her to live outside the oppressive force of the Malinche myth. Alarcón (1983) reminds us that Malinche, the actual *historical* figure, was "doomed to live in ch ins" (187). The mythologization of her as traitor assumes that she lived in a context where she could have chosen *not* to be a slave to Cortés. By the time of Barceló's great economic, personal, and community success, the forces of colonialism had already doomed the southwestern United States to Euro-American dominance. Barceló's strategy for survival and prosperity could be read as an exertion of existential freedom that benefited greatly the immediate life and well-being of her community.

This is not to suggest that Martínez should have adopted Barceló's strategies or vice versa. But it is to suggest that simply juxtaposing the two as loyal-nationalist versus complicitous-assimilator hinders our ability to comprehend the totality of circumstances in which each of these figures engaged in their circumstances of struggle. On what criteria should we judge the choices of these two figures? In describing the historical circumstances in which Barceló and Martínez came to live and struggle in the southwestern United States, I wish to emphasize certain patterns that can also be identified with the emergence of the contemporary Chicana lesbian. I turn now to this discussion.

CHERRÍE MORAGA: A CONTEMPORARY CHICANn LESBIAN

In the same way that the male myth of La Malir he serves the interests of men by making women's sexuality inherently suspect (ready to serve the interests of the conquerors), so too do descriptions of Barceló that quickly dismiss her as a "complicitous-assimilator" prohibit our understanding of her own powerfulness as a woman and entrepreneur; it also prohibits our understanding of the ways in v ich she might very well have created the conditions for a more sustained survival of her community and culture.

It is just this accusation of assimilation that functions in many debates in the contemporary struggle for racial and ethnic freedom in the United States today. The situation of the contemporary Chicana lesbian problematizes the notion at "assimilation" toward the dominant culture is de facto complicitous against the interests of Chicana and Chicano culture in the U.S. American context. The experiences of Cherríe Moraga, a contemporary self-declared Chicana lesbian, illustrate this point. The sexism and heterosexism within her mestizo/Chicano community are precisely what led her away from identifications with that community. Moraga (1983) writes,

> I gradually became anglocized because I thought it was the only option available to me toward gaining autonomy as a person without being sexually stigmatized. I can't say it was conscious at the time, only that at each juncture in my development, I instinctively made choices which I thought would allow me greater freedom of movement in the future. (174)

Situated between cultures, recognizing the dangers for herself by virtue of the heterosexism retained within her most intimate groups of association, the Chicana lesbian moves toward the dominant racist culture. The conditions for this movement toward dominant culture are in fact set up by racism.[10] Taught to hide her Mexican heritage, to speak English, and to become educated in white-dominated schools and that her light skin was an advantage for her all signified a moving up in socioeconomic class from the struggles of her parents (and mother especially) (Moraga 1983). Recognizing her sexual attraction to women and the dangers of that expression within her family and the Chicano community simply impels her in directions already set up as (racist) normative despite the known risks. Moraga the person exists in a state of incessant conflict for her conscious recognition that all her choices put her at risk. Consider, for example, the divided desires expressed by Moraga (1986)

> During the late 60s and early 70s, I was not an active part of la causa. I never managed to get myself to walk in the marches in East Los Angeles (I merely watched from the sidelines); I never went to one meting of MECHA on campus. No soy tonta. I would have been murdered in El Movimiento—light skinned, unable to speak Spanish well enough to hang; miserably attracted to women and fighting it; and constantly questioning all authority, including men's. I felt I did not belong there. (183)[11]

In order to decide that one does "not belong there," one must have necessarily been considering whether one *could* belong there. Watching "from the sidelines," anticipating how one would be received, and noticing the differences between the self and this group of identification—these are precisely the conditions of a "borderland" existence in which competing interests are at work *regardless of which position one consciously chooses to take at any given moment.* This is why the simple binarism that poses "assimilation" versus "loyalty" is insufficient for understanding the deployment of racism or the assertion of existential freedom in this context.[12]

This condition of marginal positionality, then, is exactly what makes it possible for Moraga to offer a different understanding of the meaning of *la causa, la familia,* and the terms of commitment to one's people. Within such an understanding it is possible that "to be critical of one's culture is not to betray that culture" (1983, 108). Thus, Moraga (1983) offers a revisioning of the family:

> Family is *not* by definition the man in a dominant position over women and children. *Familia* is cross-generational bonding, deep emotional ties between opposite sexes, and within our own sex. It is our sexuality, which involves, but is not limited to, intercourse or orgasm. It springs forth from touch, constant and daily. The ritual of kissing and the sign of the cross with every coming and going from the home. It is finding *familia* among friends where blood ties are formed through suffering and celebration shared. (111)[13]

It is also from this position that Moraga takes feminism to task both for both its heterosexism and its racism: "In failing . . . to take race, ethnicity, class into account in determining where women are sexually, many feminists have created an analysis of sexual oppression (often confused with sexuality itself) which is a political dead-end" (1983, 128).

Thus, we can see how one contemporary Chicana lesbian takes account of her own concrete practices and life choices through the intricately textured presence of historical pasts as she identifies them in her conscious experience, something that is also a common feature in contemporary Chicana literature (Rebolledo and Rivero 1983). For the Chicana lesbian, such a taking up of these life choices emerges from her understanding of how her sexuality positions her as an outsider (if not traitor) to her people. While sexuality becomes a key factor in the understanding of her outsider position, the racism and classism that situate her prior to her understanding of heterosexism creates a natural move toward white culture (revealing its inherent racism, the bleaching effect of the "melting pot"). The Chicana lesbian is posed against herself from within and thus comes to occupy borderlands where she is neither here nor there, where she is nowhere.[14]

BEGINNING A SELF-REFLEXIVE INTERROGATION

How are we to read the legacy of Malintzin Tenepal, Barceló, and others like them? What is "their" presence in the hearts and minds of "their" descendants?[15] If success within a socioeconomic world or safety for the expression of one's lesbianism requires a homogenization of cultural differences, then how are we to judge decisions by Mexican Americans like Moraga (and my father) to become "Anglocized"? As a collusion? As a sellout? As a commitment to survival for oneself and one's family?

I have been attempting to engage these very questions through a consideration of the past historical presences and racist-cultural context in which contemporary Chicana lesbians trace their own struggles of consciousness and experience. The selections of figures and circumstances I have made for consideration are not arbitrary but are reflexive with my own experiences and struggles. In tracing the histories of female figures in the history of the land on which they struggle, Chicana lesbians reveal these struggles as lived on their bodies and especially in their sexuality. Standing outside looking in, considering the possibilities and hoping against and within the conflicts of complex situations, the Chicana lesbian moves haltingly, freezes, and breaks away to make a small movement here or there. These are bodily lived experiences that are entirely connected to the communities and histories in which Chicana lesbians live. They portend possibilities of radical transformation for both the self and the social world (resistant though it is). Yet this portention of radical transformation occurs precisely because Chicana lesbians occupy a place of radical ambiguity where they recognize their participation in systems of domination even as they struggle against domination. Chicana lesbians trace a history that is inscribed on their own bodies as those who have been the geographical and psychical objects of colonization—a circumstance that continues to this day.

The communicative and discursive sites that establish the parameters that make the emergence of the self-declared Chicana lesbian possible, therefore, necessarily involve self-alienation for the person located in such sites. In the midst of this self-alienation, the self-declared Chicana lesbian embraces this identity precisely because it prevents her from being fully situated here or there. Such a move creates the possibilities for new kinds of self-consciousness—a strategic move that is consistent with those of the "subaltern" described by Spivak (1988):

> It is within the framework of a strategic interest in the self-alienating displacing move of and by a consciousness of collectivity, then, that self-determination and an unalienated self-consciousness can be broached. (206)

Considered according to the work and experiences of Chicana lesbians, such a broaching of unalienated self-consciousness seems to be always that, a *broaching*. This position of movement that remains a broaching thus appears as an essential location that produces the Chicana lesbian; it is, then, a position of radical ambiguity lived in the body. Jane Gallop similarly embraces the situation of an unalienated self-consciousness as always broached but never fully achieved when she says, "Identity must be continually assumed and immediately called into question" (cited in Fuss 1989, 104). What Gallop embraces as practice Chicana lesbians demonstrate by their existence in a racist-sexist-heterosexist culture. These considerations of the construction of the Chicana lesbian focus our attention on consciousness in the narrow and situated (*not* the transcendental) sense (Spivak 1988, 204) in which the assumption and questioning of identity occurs simultaneously.

THEORETICAL AND METHODOLOGICAL IMPLICATIONS

Given my own situation as a Chicana lesbian academic who has come to academic practice and feminist theorizing *precisely because* it offers me the opportunity to consider these issues as I have encountered them throughout my life, the *only* way I can engage the work of Chicana lesbians is through a very particular kind of identification. It is an identification of living within conflicting interests, an identification of difference and alienation emanating from a number of (apparent) sources and locations; it is an identification made possible through the reversibility of human perception and expression—that is, through human communication.

The move to foreground personal experience in considering my work in this chapter (as in the whole of the work) is *not* part of an effort to privilege personal experience as definitive of some "identity" (Chicana lesbian) that occupies me as subject matter deserving of exploration.[16] Rather, I use my personal experiences—as all (good) theorists and researchers do—as offering moments of initial insight, glimpses that then require sustained attention beyond the situation and circumstances in which those glimpses appeared. As I engage this sustained attention, "glimpses" continue to appear. It is this inherently reflexive interrogation and reinterrogation of moments of experiences of consciousness that allows the theorist to *realize* the ways in which an engagement in human communication allows one to *actualize* the forces and functions of discourse as situator of subject/author.[17] But one should not understand these movements of self-reflexivity as occurring within a consciousness that is separate from a world. To the contrary, the situated historical consciousness we are interested in cannot make these moves *except* as it exists in a relationship to the world made possible by an intersubjective subjectivity—that is, a subjectivity that is possible only by virtue of the intersubjective conditions of communicative praxis. As an essential feature of the location that produces the

Chicana lesbian, the condition of self-reflexivity entails within it certain dispositions useful for theory and methodology that are interested in transformations beyond oppression. Because consciousness does not exist separate from the social and cultural world, a reflexive interrogation of it necessarily involves the specification of the relationship between one's location and one's very apprehension of consciousness. The location from which the self comes to adopt the label of Chicana lesbian is an inherently contradictory one that creates a radically and ontologically contingent ambiguity.

Such an insistence on self-reflexivity constitutes a "repetition of method" consistent with Merleau-Ponty's *radical cogito*. As Lanigan (1988) puts it, the *radical cogito* is a process of "reversibility, of converting consciousness into experience and vice-versa" (14). Or, understood in a context of deconstruction, self-reflexivity as "repetition of method" can be described as a questioning the "authority of the investigating subject without paralyzing [her or] him, persistently transforming conditions of impossibility into possibility" (Spivak 1988, 201).

The persistent "transforming of conditions of impossibility into possibility" might be another way of describing the movement of consciousness engaged by Sandoval (1991) in her description of a common "U.S. third world feminist" consciousness that has emerged precisely because of its exclusion from the discourse of feminist theory. The location and production of the Chicana lesbian are consistent with Sandoval's theorizations. Sandoval describes "U.S. third world feminism" as representing "a form of historical consciousness whose very structure lies outside the conditions of possibility which regulate the oppositional expressions of dominant feminism" (1991, 1). Sandoval delineates this historical consciousness *topographically*, as a surface that the "U.S. third world feminist" negotiates *differentially*, shifting from one position to another as she moves in and out of feminist contexts which display varying degrees of white hegemony (1991, 11). In this differential consciousness, the Chicana lesbian, like Sandoval's "U.S. third world feminist," lives a radical ambiguity where she is always posed to herself as never fully here nor there. An interrogation of the location of the production of the Chicana lesbian therefore provides a means by which this radical ambiguity might in fact provide the impetus for radical transformations precisely because of the essential undecidability of her positionality. Such a position requires the kind of theoretical movements described by Butler (1993):

> The task is to refigure this necessary "'outside'" as a future horizon, one in which the violence of exclusion is perpetually in the process of being overcome. But of equal importance is the preservation of the outside, the site where discourse meets its limits, where the opacity of what is not

included in a given regime of truth acts as a disruptive set of linguistic impropriety and unrepresentability, illuminating the violent and contingent boundaries of that normative regime precisely through the inability of that regime to represent that which might pose a fundamental threat to its continuity. (53)

Enacting these theoretical movements is not simply an abstract theoretical endeavor; rather, it is always already lived—and must be engaged as—on the bodies of those occupying the topographies of contested lands where the material (geographical) and psychical struggles entail radical shifts in apprehension and understanding of one's circumstance so that one broaches but never achieves an unalienated self-consciousness.

CONCLUSION

The presence of historical pasts through which I have considered the production of the Chicana lesbian has involved a focus on ambiguous figures who have been refigured by Chicana lesbian (and Chicana) writers so as to create space for transformations in meaning and practice *for themselves*. In their work, Chicana lesbians like Cherríe Moraga reveal themselves also as ambiguous figures *to themselves*. Deeply entwined within racist, sexist, heterosexist, and classist formations that pit them against themselves, other women, and their ethnic/racial communities, these Chicana lesbians attain agency by engaging these conflicting forces, yet always in a contingent and ambiguous way.

It is this condition of contingency and ambiguity that challenges static notions of "assimilationist versus nationalist" and "complicitous-traitor versus loyal-culturalist" binarisms. It also suggests the necessity of self-reflexivity in academic work that purports to challenge the oppression and hegemony entailed in academic institutions. By her very existence, the Chicana lesbian embodies a radical ambiguity that requires a continual reengagement in subject position and its relation to the historical and cultural dimensions of the position—borderland. I have suggested that it is precisely the contingency and radical ambiguity of her borderland subjectivity that creates the possibilities for radical transformation.

In the next chapter, I turn to a consideration of how precisely the possibilities for radical transformation are taken up and actualized in the intrasubjective and intersubjective world of the Chicana lesbian and others who are the objects of oppression. As we have seen in this chapter, the ambiguity of the Chicana lesbian's position relative to the dominant culture and her Chicano culture and even within *la familia* creates a precarious situation where resistance against cultural norms marks her as disloyal but where adherence to them can lead to self-hate. The Chicana lesbian exists in a double bind where she is at risk regardless of which choices she makes. Because she exists in the context of racist-sexist-heterosexist-classist cultures, the Chicana lesbian, like all those who are the objects of oppression, is at risk for internalizing the damaging messages about herself carried by the dominant culture and even within her own familial relationships. My effort in the next chapter, then, is to consider how it is possible for the Chicana lesbian to move out from under these oppressive forces and transform her intra- and intersubjective existence into conditions relatively free of the oppressive forces by which she is otherwise surrounded.

NOTES

1. It is important to note that although I am using the language "the Chicana lesbian," I do not intend to suggest that there is such a thing as *the* Chicana lesbian—presumably a person or group of persons who share a common ancestry and same-sex sexual orientation. Rather, I focus on "the Chicana lesbian" as a label for self-naming that becomes available within a complex and varying set of social, cultural, and historical circumstances. No label is capable of containing all that may come to fall under it. I am addressing the emergence of "the Chicana lesbian" as a possibility tied to specific and concrete circumstances of lived experience and social becoming. The label itself cannot substitute as an account of that experience or becoming. There is great diversity among those who would adopt the label "Chicana lesbian," and there are certainly many other ways of talking about or representing "Chicana lesbian" (e.g., Trujillo 1991). My work here does not intend to homogenize this group. I am interested, however, in tracing though the work of contemporary Chicanas and Chicana lesbians in order to evoke histories and circumstances that participate in one kind of emergence for the Chicana lesbian today—there needs to be many works that take up this effort.

2. See also García (1989), Moraga and Anzaldúa (1983), and Anzaldúa (1987, 1990).

3. See Ruiz (1993) for an excellent discussion of the pressures of Americanization faced by young Mexican American women in the Southwest between 1920 and 1950. While aspirations for economic success were often embraced by these young people, such success *required* Americanization. Even while these young women retained strong senses of their own ethnic heritage, their efforts to move up the socioeconomic ladder was so besieged with racism and their life world so besieged with "American images" that despite their own sense of cultural self, they were forced to adopt the outward signs of "white American" as prerequisites for success. Ruiz's essay offers examples that especially "hit home" for me given that my father, who was born into deep poverty in 1928 in McAllen, Texas (in the southern tip of Texas), grew up during this time and faced many of the same circumstances described by Ruiz. His own stories told to me about his childhood resonate in the stories told by Ruiz.

4. See Alarcón (1990). Sandoval (1991) illustrates this point specifically within feminist academic theorizing since the late 1970s.

5. On the importance of locatedness in academic theorizing, see Alcoff (1992). Following from Lanigan, I use the words *self-reflexive, critical,* and *analytic* to denote theoretical movements that take the researcher/theorist in situ as problematic and thus engage in a turning back on the conditions of production (self-reflexive) by using criteria that are alternatively determined as necessary or sufficient for those conditions; these are the first steps of an eidetic application of semiotic phenomenology (see Lanigan 1988; 1991; 1992, appendix B).

6. See Giddings (1984) and Cott (1987) for discussions of the history of anti-black racism within the women's movement since the late nineteenth century. Both texts expose racist practices among white women that continue to exist today. See García (1989) for a discussion of the common expressions of racism encountered by Chicanas, Asian, and black American women in feminist academic work during the 1970s. I do not mean to suggest that any of these three sites is static or by some essential condition necessarily a site of exclusion for the Chicana lesbian. To the contrary, certainly within the Chicano movement, the work of the National Association of Chicano Studies has, over the past several years, engaged issues of sexism directly; the establishment of Mujeres Activas en Letras y Cambio Social (MALCS) in 1983 draws "from a tradition of political struggle" and is "dedicated to the documentation, analysis, and interpretation of the Chicana/Latina experience in the United States" (de la Torre and Pesquera 1993, 5). But the actual effects of these changes, the extent to which they are precursors for transformations in discursive formations, is unknowable as yet. Regardless, the history that allows us to see the discursive formations that situate the Chicana lesbian as an exclusion is clear and therefore also present even as processes of transformation may be enacting.

7. For discussions regarding this particular function of groups, see Lanigan (1988, 203–222; 1992, appendix D), McFeat (1974), and Reusch and Bateson (1987).

8. Within Mexican culture, "Malinche" is a name that has a history of being used as an insult to both men and women. There is evidence that the actual woman who assisted Cortéz in the conquest was named Malinali (González 2000). Doña Marina was the name given to her by the Spanish. See Cypress (1991) for a discussion of Malinali as a figure in Mexican literature.

9. For a discussion of the difference between "good" and "bad" ambiguity, see Lanigan (1988, 3–18). See also Bateson's work on the double bind (1972, 271–278).

10. See Gordon (1995) for an analysis of bad faith as it informs the racist minds and practices that produce the systems and structures that maintain cultural racisms. Such an analysis demands a shift from considering racism on an individual level to its very situation in the social world: "The task, in short, is to address the problems between society and the self, the problem of socially situated existence under the force of institutional sites of power or terror. This is precisely the point of examining racism from the standpoint of bad faith: one must address the transcendent and factical dimensions of human reality as a situated reality" (72).

11. Ana Castillo (1994) makes a similar point, though she did participate in El Movimiento: "As a political activist from El Movimiento Chicano/Latino, I had come away from it with a great sense of despair as a woman. Inherent to my despair, I felt, was my physiology that was demeaned, misunderstood, objectified, and excluded by the politic of those men with whom I had aligned myself on the basis of our mutual subjugation as Latinos in the United States" (24).

12. bell hooks (1990, 29) makes a similar point in the context of the essentialism/constructivism debate in black academic and nonacademic worlds.

13. See Audre Lorde (1984) for a similar re-visioning of the possibilities for the place of erotic-emotional bonds as they relate to spiritual and political transformation.

14. Note that the word *nowhere* is both *no-where* and *now-here*. For an informative discussion of the methodological implications of Foucault's "rhetoric of the person situated in discourse," see Lanigan (1992), "Somebody Is Nowhere: Michel Foucault on Rhetoric and the Discourse of Subjectivity in the Human Sciences" (81–113).

15. It is very important to *not* make generalizations about some group of people arbitrarily designated "Mexican Americans." Migration to the United States from Mexico has been and continues to be an always present phenomenon. First-, second-, and third-generation (and beyond) migrants have widely differing experiences. The socioeconomic class of immigrants also makes profound differences. My effort in this work is to focus on those "Americans" who have never been "immigrants," whose ancestry on the land of the southwestern United States pre-dates 1848. Yet this is not to claim some sort of "authenticity" based on this equally arbitrary designation. It does, however, situate myself (this is heritage of my father) relative to this academic-activist effort and begins to lay the ground for directing my interrogations precisely on the conditions of its production.

16. See Fuss (1989, 97–112) for an informative discussion of "identity politics."

17. See Lanigan (1992, appendix B).

4

LA CONCIENCIA DE LA MESTIZA: INTRA- AND INTERSUBJECTIVE TRANSFORMATIONS OF RACIST AND HOMOPHOBIC CULTURE

> She has discovered that she can't hold concepts or ideas in rigid boundaries. The border and walls that are supposed to keep the undesirable ideas out are entrenched habits and patterns of behavior; these patterns and habits are the enemy within.
>
> —Gloria Anzaldúa

Persons who are racially and sexually marked within the dominant culture—who are seen as embodying or having the potential to embody deviancy and difference—are in a position of either (1) internalizing cultural norms which dehumanize their existence or (2) consciously battling them. The line between these two responses, however, is often unclear. Assimilation, for example, is a survival strategy that sometimes works by creating better chances for movement up the socioeconomic ladder of U.S. American society. Children learn to speak English as a native language, gain access to education, and are able to aspire to (and sometimes achieve) a place fully within the mainstream of culture. Despite such an achievement, however, a person who remains marked, especially by skin color, is always at risk for being stereotyped by racist norms. Moreover, it is also possible that even in the best-case assimilation scenario, children learn to feel a sense of superiority over those others who have not assimilated so well or to be shamed by their parents' lack of schooling or poor economic standing. Such a child learns to separate the world into the "good" and the "bad" Mexicans (or blacks and so on). Racist assimilation encourages these divisions according to heavily stereotyped and racist notions about people of color. In so doing, a racist-assimilationist culture discourages persons from recognizing the ways in which racist practices (carried by virtue of racist stereotypes, racialized knowledge, and so on) are a common enemy. Instead, divisions are perpetuated among people who are subjected to the same racializations but who bear those racializations to different degrees. When these divisions, orchestrated by a racist-assimilationist culture, take hold, the racist norms informing those divisions remain unseen, free from critique, and therefore perpetuate themselves in the personal, social, and cultural worlds of persons, groups, and institutions.

To the degree that the normative standards of the dominant culture are *not* critiqued or called into question is the degree to which persons will replicate them. When those normative standards are racist-sexist-heterosexist-classist, those normative standards will be internalized even (perhaps especially) by those who are targeted by those standards. By virtue of our inextricable being-in-communication-with, most of us begin life internalizing cultural norms and developing sedimented habits or dispositions that will tend to reinforce the narrow terms of normalcy provided by culture.

By virtue of our inextricable being-in-communication-with, the normative conditions of our cultural time and place will necessarily be internalized as our own disposition toward self, others, and the world. Recognizing the ways in which our very disposition toward ourselves, others, and the world entails a negative internalization is a prerequisite for freeing oneself from the ongoing internalization of the oppressive force of the negative stereotypes. Success in this battle results in a creation of inter-subjective space where the dehumanizing effects of cultural oppression are transformed and possibilities for new *intra*subjectivities emerge. How, specifically, are successful battles against racist and homophobic culture waged? How should we assess the achievement of a person's intra-subjective humanization in relation to the intrinsically racist and homo-phobic forces carried *inter*subjectively within Anglo culture? How do we understand the battles of lived experience against internalized oppression in relation to the structural and semiotic system that maintains Anglo culture as racist and homophobic? What is the point of conjunction (border/*frontera*) between the Othered person and the racist culture where oppression and dehumanization are generated and/or subverted?

In addressing these questions I take Gloria Anzaldúa's *la conciencia de la mestiza* as thematic—that is, as offering a viable theory and methodology capable of transforming the forces of the dominant culture and engendering a humanizing consciousness that has the capacity to break free from the otherwise deadening forces of a racist, sexist, and homophobic culture. In selecting Anzaldúa's *la conciencia de la mestiza* as thematic, I will be following her own traversals through the multidimensional world of borderlands. My effort is to offer additional theoretical and material flesh on the embodied presence already in view in Anzaldúa's *la conciencia de la mestiza*. My aim is to explicate the features and functions of a humanizing consciousness rooted concretely in the lived ambiguities of daily life that also maintains a necessary historical and political critique of the dehumanizing forces within the dominant European and Anglo cultural worlds. In focusing on sexual and ethnic oppressions, I hope to identify a nexus of intersecting pressures that create certain boundaries and thus also certain possibilities for human becoming, for the emergence of different kinds of conscious awareness, and thus also for various transformations in the material, communicative, and intersubjective worlds within which all human beings are situated. This effort leads me to focus on the role of a critical consciousness in the process of transforming oppressive inter-subjective norms and its relationship to the descriptive effort taken in the focus on the lived body as the point of an irreducible being-in-communi-cation-with. I illustrate this relation between critical consciousness and lived body with an analysis of sexual and ethnic reversals in the emergence of new consciousness.

ANZALDÚA'S *LA CONCIENCIA DE LA MESTIZA*

Entering into a consideration of Anzaldúa's work must begin with a strong caution as to how it should *not* be used. Although I am offering *la conciencia de la mestiza* as a way of successfully fighting battles against the ongoing internalization of a racist and homophobic culture, it should not be used like the latest recipe on how to achieve success or as an ac-tivity one might take up to overcome the difficulties of a given day. This is because the theoretical effort can never be equated to practice. The theoretical effort itself does not entail a one-to-one correspondence be-tween the ideas carried therein and the manifestation of those ideas in the concrete world of human experience. Thus, it is important to understand how Anzaldúa got to her theorizing, to take up not only the principles of her theoretical positions but also the very movement of her thinking and experiencing through which she came to them. Approaching theory—es-pecially a theory portending liberation—in this way gives us pause even in nominating a solution. There is a kind of solution here, but it must not be considered a solution with an end point. We do better to take it as a solution that now begs questions of how exactly in this time and place, with what set of social and historical circumstances, and in conjunction with what people, what place, what issues, what ideas. It is important to work against the tendency to simplify, gloss over, or to too quickly valo-rize the "new consciousness" without committing oneself to the complex-ity and gut-wrenching struggle out of which theorizing like Anzaldúa's is born. Without a commitment to engaging the complexity and struggle at the level of the lived body in our own lives and work, we run the risk of taking the insights born of gut-wrenching struggle and making them into a high-flying flashy theory by which we may travel a long way on a safe and clear highway while those from whom we have taken those insights remain walking the bruising pavement of the neighborhood streets.[1]

This necessarily dangerous predicament of doing theory is, in fact, characteristic of what Chicana theorist Chela Sandoval (1991) identifies as the work of "hegemonic feminist scholars" of the 1980s who "produced the histories of feminist consciousness which they believed to typify the modes of exchange operating within the oppositional spaces of the women's movement" (5). In taking up this effort, (white) feminist scholars constructed "typologies, systematic classifications of all possible forms of feminist praxis" that became the "official stories by which the white women's movement understands itself and its interventions in history." Although the work of U.S. women of color was not ignored in these theoretical efforts, they were often simply added in or characterized as "mere description"—in other words, not considered seriously in their own terms or as a challenge to the very self-understanding that feminist theory was taking of itself (Sandoval 1991, 5; see also Alarcón 1990, 356–369). Essential insights emerging from the work of U.S. women of color were thus lost even while the theoretical effort taken up by the dominant feminist scholars seemed to include their work. While dominant U.S. feminism began to look to work by U.S. women of color, it tended to miss the significance of the work and failed to recognize the powerful theoretical insights and unique form of consciousness present in the very movement of U.S. women of color.[2] The attention to the embodied flesh that is the substance and methodology of much of Chicana feminist theorizing must not be theorized away in abstract language that allows for a distanced and removed engagement. Such a commitment to the embodied flesh must take seriously the material contact of the lived body in its position as anchor within the lived world. It is here that the possibilities for meaningfulness become actualized preconsciously and may thus also be made available for transformations of the very (noetic) mode through which one apprehends the world. One may not yet be consciously aware of what is present at the level of the lived body, but a commitment to experience at this level raises our capacity to interrogate the very possibilities of our coming to new consciousness. It is here that efforts of transformation in consciousness must be located.

Gloria Anzaldúa's (1987, 77–98) *la conciencia de la mestiza* is a description of a successful struggle against the oppressive forces of the dominant culture at the level of the lived body. Her work provides a set of circumstances and practices through which we might create humanizing spaces in our cultural, social, and personal worlds alike. Yet, because it is attentive to the particularities of situation and the possibilities of the lived body, Anzaldúa's work cannot be reduced to a prescription, a set of procedures, or a single perspective that can be copied as a way to achieve liberating transformations for the self and the social world. *La conciencia de la mestiza* is a "consciousness of the borderlands" and a "struggle of borders." Such a struggle is marked by perplexity, internal strife, and psychic restlessness resulting from the "clash of voices" and uncertainty as to "which collectivity" one should listen to. The mestiza is a hybrid, situated between cultures, languages, communities, and histories, with each foot set on conflicting and incompatible sides.

The messages, codes, and socially encouraged self-understandings taken up from each side of the border present for the hybrid are often conflicting and never fully compatible and thus create a state of constant transition and negotiation between these often opposing positions. *La conciencia de la mestiza* exists in a state of inner struggle at the level of the lived body and its capacity to make perception expression and expression perception. "You are the darker other, you are dirty, you are poor, you can't speak, your desires are sick, you deserve to be at the bottom." To the extent that I hear you (the anonymous voice) say these things and understand them to be about me is the extent to which they are already part of me and my body as I live moment by moment in the world. Yet there are other voices coming through. I counter, "But I love, I am proud, I have dignity, I know you are wrong. I know you are evil, the one who cannot love, the one who projects his own fear and inadequacy upon my darker woman body because it is powerful and you cannot control or own it. I declare war on you. I shall seek you out in every crevice, in every thread of thought and moment of feeling. I shall root you out and destroy you, kill your presence within me, separate myself from your reaches and all that you are."[3]

Taking up a counterstance in the flesh and against one side of the conflicting voices is a necessary first step option for *la mestiza*. But it is an option that locks the person into mortal and violent battle where one remains equally circumscribed by the dominant discourse as before—one now explicitly fights against what used to be accepted preconsciously, yet the terms remain the same. Taking the counterstance is necessary to the extent that it forces our engagement with the flesh of the lived body and its shared material contact with the world. But, Anzaldúa tells us, it cannot be a way of life.[4] At some point we must cross sides, stop simply reacting, and engage the struggle from the place of being on both shores at once. In this way it is possible, although painful and troubling, to engage all the parts of ourselves, embracing all the histories and struggles that make up our voices and the substance of our lived bodies. Living in a racist and homophobic world makes our existence an inner war at the level of the preconscious, where the very mode of our perception and expression achieves its direction and shape.[5] It is a struggle of the flesh, of that contact between my lived body and the general momentum of the social and historical world carried intersubjectively in the sedimented meanings of language, the habits of movement through time and space and the shared material nature of body and objects. *La mestiza* recognizes the direct conflicts at work at the level of her lived body, in her own perception of herself and world, and the dangers of retaining those sedimented (racist and homophobic) meanings carried intersubjectively from one side or the other of the border she bridges.

Living on both sides at once, acting and not reacting, commits *la mestiza* to open possibilities through uncharted space where conflicting possibilities for communication and points of possible meaningfulness remain. I see you seeing me. I see you seeing me seeing you. What do I see? I used to be able to take all this for granted. But now I must ask, Who am I when I see you seeing me see you? What are borders between us? How am I crossing them? How are you crossing them? Who do I listen to? From the perspective of which of my communities do I respond now? Borders that were previously clear and distinct now blur, and separations become less clear. I must develop a tolerance for ambiguity and contradiction. There is a constant shifting at the level of "habitual formations." In working at the level of the lived body to create a synthesis, *la mestiza* works at the level of praxis carried by the reversibility of our perception and expression, thus creating "a third element . . . a new consciousness." A "source of intense pain," this process is also a "continual creative motion that keeps breaking down the unitary aspect" of each particular moment of lived experience (Anzaldúa 1987, 80).

The mestiza has her own way of successful struggle against the internalization of oppression (*el camino de la mestiza*). The first step is to take inventory, to see what we have inherited from our ancestors—Native, Mexican, Anglo. The goal is to "put history through a sieve, winnow out lies, look at the forces we as a race, as women, have been part of" (Anzaldúa 1987, 82). *La mestiza* makes "a conscious rupture with all oppressive traditions of all cultures and religions" (Anzaldúa 1987, 82). It is a conscious rupture achieved through a concrete practice of explicitly recognizing, acknowledging, and demanding that our newly come-to understandings become part of the live meeting of persons and ideas in the very living worlds we inhabit—not simply a counterattack against those (people or culture) who are perceived to have done harm to us but a practice that simultaneously demands that we interrogate ourselves at the level of the preconscious possibilities carried by lived bodies and thus create different possibilities of the meaningfulness of our lives. Communicate that rupture as it is lived on and in your body. Document the struggle. Become a new perspective. Recognize where racial shame, loss of dignity, and respect create insecurity and an effort to overcome through a false sense of power. Recognize this source of abuse whether by the hand of men (li ' or dark) or the reaches of a culture. Demand admission and testimony that they have done violence, have made wounds, and have caused damage. Demand acknowledgment that they are afraid of power. Demand that they recognize that the racial other is their double, their shadow projection. Demand that they acknowledge their rejection of you, dark woman. Recognize the power and possibility of being "crossers." Understand courageousness of queer crossers—the ones who tread the dangerous borders of sexuality. Recognize how the queer's expression ("deviancy") of sexuality is already a perceptive capacity that reaches far beyond those who are unable to cross this border. Recognize the alliances to be forged from the reach and expanse traveled by the queer of color crosser. Acknowledge diversity among your own, your own queer. Be true to your face. Understand how "the dominant white culture is killing us slowly with its ignorance," its hidden weapons, and its whitewash of our history (Anzaldúa 1987, 86). We need to know history of many people and their struggles, and they need to know ours. Make a commitment to persons, their lived bodies, and their many histories. Let us take inventory and be true to our face.

TAKING INVENTORY, BEING TRUE TO YOUR FACE

Documenting, exposing, and demanding recognition of the damages done by virtue of racist cultural perceptions carried across generations is an essential part of *la mestiza*'s taking inventory. For the contemporary Chicana, this documentation of damages done requires a reconsideration of the "making of America" and the destruction exacted against native cultures and people who, across generations, continued to identify with native culture. Such an effort exposes what is at essence a racist logic that leads the European conquistadors and priests—Franciscan, Dominican, and Jesuit—to consider themselves not only superior but to have an incontestable rightness to dominate and destroy the darker and racialized Other they encounter in the "new world." Even the most humane among the Europeans who traveled to the American continent were equal participants in the destruction of the native people and their cultures. Bartolomé de Las Casas, the great defender of the native people, was, in the end, incapable stopping the violence and destruction waged on them. His very belief in the native people's capacity for faith (which he grasped much better than Cortés) became an adequate basis for their destruction. Las Casas differed radically from Hernán Cortés, whose sole purpose was conquest. Las Casas, for example, argues "against the *repartimiento*, the feudal cession of the Indians to the Spaniards, which Cortés . . . promotes" (Todorov 1984, 176). And yet, in the end, both Las Casas and Cortés are in agreement "on one essential point: the subjugation of America to Spain, the annexation of the Indians to Christian religion, the preference for colonialism over enslavement" (177).

The European effort to colonize the people and cultures of the Americas was motivated by a clear recognition that "colonialism is more efficient than enslavement" in the conquering of a culture. The ultimate purpose of the Spanish invaders is the obliteration of the native culture and the replacement of it with their own. They prefer to do this through "conversion." Such a conversion is, of course, facilitated by the conqueror's ability to understand and communicate with the native culture—the Spanish aim to understand so as to be able to destroy through communication (a violence that avoids bloody battles). Despite great appreciation for many aspects of the Aztec culture, Cortés and Las Casas, like Columbus before them, admire only at the level of object. As Todorov (1992) puts it, "Cortés goes into ecstasies about the Aztec production but does not acknowledge their markers as human individualities to be set on the same level as himself" (129). The collection of Aztec artifacts, the exploitation of their people, and the assumption of European cultural superiority all fuel an attitude justifying forced assimilation, which, it can be argued, has been maintained even to this very day. According to Todorov (1984), "Since the period of the conquest, for almost 350 years, Western Europe has tried to assimilate the Other, to do away with an exterior alterity, and has in great part succeeded. Its way of life and its values have spread around the world; as Columbus wished, the colonized people have adopted European customs and have put on clothes" (247–248).

One of the consequences of genocide is the destruction not only of a culture and its people but also of any records or evidence of it from their own perspective. We will never know what the conquest was like from the native people's point of view. Yet this point of view is important because of the way it marks the borders across which Anzaldúa and other women of color work. We can fill in this side of the border by looking to the work of Frantz Fanon. Born in Martinique in 1925; educated in France, where he studied psychiatry and philosophy; and spending many years working as a psychiatrist in Algeria, Fanon gives us what is perhaps one of the most insightful accounts of the experience of the racialized Other made object by a dominating and racist European culture. In bold and unevasive language, Fanon (1967) says, "However painful it may be for me to accept this conclusion, I am obliged to state it: for the black man there is only one destiny. And it is white" (10). In explaining how it is that for the black man—and the marked darker other generally—there is only one destiny and it is white, Fanon undertakes what he considers a basically psychological study. Yet he immediately notes that the psychological alienation experienced by the person of color is at once also social and economic.

Whatever "'inferiority complexes'" come to live within the psyches of people of color it is a result of a process of social and economic factors becoming "internalized" or, better, "epidermalized." "It will be seen," as Fanon (1967) states, "that the black man's alienation is not an individual question" (11). To propose a psychological study of persons of color must by necessity be a study of the social and cultural world within which they live. It is from this point of view, then, that we can begin to connect the fact of an oppressive, assimilationist, massacre-oriented and racist European culture with lived flesh-and-body experience of those who are the objects of that oppressive culture. It is this conjunction, border, or *frontera* between a free human being and the dehumanizing effect of an oppressive cultural system where we will find both the generation and the subversion of oppression. This border, *frontera*, is material, epidermal, lived in the flesh, and suffused through all modes of communication and ultimately the very terms of intersubjective existence. By analyzing what he takes to be a "massive psychoexistential complex" created by the "juxtaposition of the white and black races," Fanon hopes to destroy it (12). Analyzing it, he must have already destroyed it for himself, even if it still exists within the dominant social, cultural, and historical world. Indeed, throughout this text, Fanon explores and explodes every fold and fiber through which a racist culture seeks to trap the person of color, leaving no place for him to see himself except as that racist culture would have him do so. It is a project that shares much with Anzaldúa's *conciencia de la mestiza* in the sense that it addresses the difference between a consciousness that remains intrasubjectively trapped within inherently racist intersubjectivities carried within the dominant culture and the consciousness that destroys that culture's capacity to circumscribe the person of color's intrasubjective coming to consciousness. Anzaldúa's effort is to address the actual concrete and embodied practices by which we can break free from the racist, sexist, and homophobic elements carried so forcefully in the colonialist and imperialist mentality—a sick mentality that defines far too much of our common history.

In a passion and boldness equal to that of Fanon's, Anzaldúa (1990) tells us that the "mestiza's dual or multiple personality is plagued by psychic restlessness" (377). But unlike Fanon, Anzaldúa does not focus so much on the psychic restlessness and being in a "state of perpetual transition" as being an inferiority complex engendered by the culture itself (although she agrees that it is). Rather, she sees these circumstances of cultural binds as moments of possibility for transformation. To live within, between, and among multiple communities of identification is to "undergo a struggle of flesh, a struggle of border, an inner war." The mestiza is in a position of cultural collision that "we see as an attack on ourselves and our beliefs as a threat and we attempt to block with a counterstance" (Anzaldúa

1987, 78). Yet she reminds us that this strategy "locks us into a mortal combat . . . where we are all reduced to the common denominator of violence" (78). "At some point," Anzaldúa says, "on our way to a new consciousness, we will have to leave the opposite bank, the split between two mortal combatants somehow healed so that we are on both shores at once, see through serpent and eagle eyes. Or perhaps we will decide to disengage from the dominant culture, write it off altogether as a lost cause and cross the border to a wholly new and separate border" (78–79). Analyzing so as to destroy the violences perpetuated by virtue of our intersubjective existence within a racist and homophobic culture requires accountability to the borders that are imposed and a recognition of our creative capacities to bridge them. Bridging those borders destroys the intersubjective violence out of which an oppressed intrasubjectivity is born and creates both an intrasubjectivity free of those violences, and the possibility of recognizing the transformations socially, culturally, and historically and thereby creating new intersubjectivities free of the deadening forces carried in the racist histories and self-understanding. "Nothing," Anzaldúa reminds us, "happens in the 'real world' unless it happens first in the images in our heads" (87).

PHENOMENOLOGICAL AND CRITICAL JUDGMENT

In both Fanon and Anzaldúa's work, the taking on of a critical judgment is a necessary first step in throwing off the intersubjective pressures that would have persons of color believing the lie of their inferiority intrasubjectively. It is also necessary that this first critical judgment identify the legacy of colonialism and imperialism for the far-reaching damages enacted on persons and cultures of color. This critical judgment must carry a historical perspective that invokes the criteria of racist assimilation, economic exploitation, as well as the sexist and homophobic norms carried therein. Having taken this critical perspective, one can then begin a full-force descriptive effort through which the particulars of a racist and homophobic culture direct their forces in the very hearts of minds of those who identified as the racial and/or sexual other within the terms of the racist and homophobic culture. Taking the critical counterstance and combining it with attention to descriptive detail of our intrasubjective existence constitutes a border crossing through which we create the capacity to change both our intrasubjective existence and the intersubjective forces that govern the general possibilities of intrasubjective becoming.

My discussions thus far reveal the ways in which crossing borders is a complex matter involving a critical examination of lived experience and the social and cultural norms that have exerted pressures on the very possibilities of a person's coming to consciousness of self and history. Ultimately, it is only by virtue of a consciously engaged critical perspective against the dominant cultural norms that we gain access to what has been always present but varyingly accessible experiences of race, ethnicity, sexuality, and class. In my own life it has been by virtue of my family's class privilege, my light color skin, and my linguistic privilege that I avoided any consciousness of being racially marked. Seeing myself primarily through the normative lens of the dominant culture allowed me to evade the persistent though barely conscious questions concerning my racial and ethnic heritage that suffused the whole of my growing-up world. As I came to recognize the ways in which my experiences were at odds with the dominant culture, an opening began to emerge through which I could take up those persistent questions regarding race and ethnicity. Thus began a sustained personal and professional endeavor to critically reconsider the present (*mi familia*) and past (history of racism and conquest) circumstances of life and the social and discursive worlds that have led me to where I have been.

In taking up this endeavor, a new and more involved critical consciousness emerges. It is a new consciousness because I had never before seen myself as a Chicana or the world from the perspective of a Chicana. After a great deal of time struggling with my own identification as a Chicana, reading the work of Chicanas and Chicana lesbians, and seeking out other Chicanas and Chicanos, I was able recognize the Chicana in myself and was therefore also able to see the world differently than I had previously. But it is also a more involved critical consciousness because during those moments in which I could see myself as a Chicana, I did not simply stop seeing the world or myself as I had previously—I could not fully step across to the other side. My coming to see the world from a Chicana perspective was an achievement made possible by critically engaging the fact of my own life within the historical context of conquest and the implications that carried for the lives of my parents, grandparents, great-grandparents, and so on. Yet that achievement could not erase my knowledge and lived experience from all those moments prior to the formation of that new critical consciousness from which I came to speak as a Chicana, nor could it inform a politics of identification that was tenable within the complexities of my everyday life experiences. Despite having attained a new consciousness as a Chicana, I retained a great deal of ambiguity about what that meant in my ordinary everyday life experience.

The autobiographical emphasis in chapter two particularly has been an essential space within which I have struggled with these conflicting and ambiguous experiences of consciousness. The phenomenological emphasis has allowed me to focus the autobiographical account on my consciousness of lived experience and identify key events that have generated my conscious awareness of race, ethnicity, cultural heritage, privilege, and power. The influence of phenomenology on chapter two is significant, yet less so than the influence of Chicana lesbian writers like Gloria Anzaldúa, Cherríe Moraga, Emma Perez, and others, whose critical perspective contextualizes their descriptive accounts of experience. Encountering the critical perspective taken by Chicana lesbians and other women of color has had a far greater effect in my developing capacity to describe my experience of race, ethnicity, and sexuality than my formal study of semiotics and phenomenology (important as that formal study has been). In reading the work of Chicana lesbians and listening to them present their work, for example, I have often experienced a kind of earth-shaking effect whereby I feel dazed, shocked, and unsure of where I am stepping and spend several days feeling reverberations from the experience complete their movement through my body—a state of perplexity about what to do with the obvious meaningfulness that these texts and speakers had for me. My study of phenomenology provoked similar, though less extreme, experiences to the extent that such study put the fact of my lived experience into question. Through my study of phenomenology I recognized that the experiences I had in my encounter with Chicana writers and speakers is precisely suited for phenomenological investigation. In making my journey through Chicana identity in chapter two, I deliberately privileged descriptions of experience that were available to me only as a result of the critical perspectives offered by Chicanas and deemphasized a formal and explicit application of a semiotic and phenomenological methodology. This privileging of experience was informed by phenomenological theory yet ironically also seemed at odds with it.

While phenomenology has provided concepts and practices around which I have been able to think about and sort through the complexities of my lived experience, phenomenological concepts themselves cannot encapsulate the particularities of experience or transformations in conscious awareness. Theoretically, phenomenology offers an understanding of the capacity of human consciousness to manifest its intentionality (lived body as anchor) and thereby the very conditions by which certain moments of consciousness are possible (see chapter one). Yet there is also a certain gap between the theoretical tools that phenomenology (or any other theory) offers and the struggles experienced in the flesh and blood, at the level of the lived body as it retains the facts of one's lived experience: No matter how insightful and potentially empowering phenomenology's focus on lived experience is, it still always requires a content, the "that" which is experienced and the social, discursive, and historical situation in which it comes to be. We may understand how oppression and transformation operate, but experiencing either or both is always bound to a "that" which is lived in experience, however momentarily or contingently.

If there is one situation that guarantees that persons living within the norms of a racist and homophobic culture will remain living within those norms, it is in the case of the internalization of racist and homophobic stereotypes.[6] The internalization of racist and homophobic stereotypes is sufficient in itself to direct people who are the objects of those stereotypes toward and into states of self-hate. The ability, therefore, to see the functioning of racist and homophobic culture, to identify oneself as one who has lived the experience of being an object of oppression by virtue of that culture, and therefore to extricate oneself at the level of the lived body from the deadening grip of internalized oppression is a prerequisite for undoing the ongoing oppression of a racist and homophobic culture. The development of this ability requires a perspective that steps outside and is critical of the dominant cultural norms. The descriptions of experience I offer in this work, for example, are postcritical awareness—that is, they begin with a critical insight about the racist, sexist, and homophobic nature of the dominant culture. In contrast, because phenomenological description can be understood as aiming to suspend all prior judgment—to describe the fullness of experience as it is experienced prior to the injunction of a critical perspective or the assumed significance of certain differences—phenomenology can be understood as incompatible with a critical-interpretive effort that *begins* with an invocation of specific critical criteria. In her own phenomenological research, for example, Sobchack (1992) resists "introducing the accepted terminology of 'sexual difference' or starting my description relying on the ground staked out by dominant theoretical discourse" (143). In this case, the "dominant theoretical discourse" is the broad area of film studies and film criticism where feminist and psychoanalytic perspectives have, at least in some circles, a certain dominance. It is against this dominance that Sobchack directs her work. She makes this choice in part because "it has seemed important to introduce the lived-body in terms of its essential ontological functions—that is, those functions that do not precede, but do provide the ground for, the marking of and discrimination against the lived-body and it excessive, ambiguous, and over-running semiosis" (1992, 144). The commonly known discriminations against the lived body (i.e., race, gender, and deformity) are made both possible (provide the ground for) and alterable by virtue of the lived body's essential ontological function of being the anchor point for the reversibility of personal perception and cultural expression (equally cultural perception and personal expression). Human communication defined by the reversibility of perception and expression entails, for Sobchack, the possibility of "a condition of mutual freedom bound in sociality and language that we do not see in the current climate of theoretical pessimism" (1992, 142). What de Lauretis (1984) says about Peirce's semiotics of habit is equally true for Sobchack's phenomenological focus on freedom in cinematic communication: "This theory of meaning does not incur the risk of idealism because the systems of systems of signs which makes human communication possible is translatable into habits, concrete action upon the world; and this action then rejoins the universe of signification by converting itself into new signs and new semiotic systems" (175).[7] The fact that some habits and sign systems are tyrannical and oppressive is not denied, yet neither is it affirmed as a "necessary or absolute *condition* of our encounter with others" (Sobchack 1992, 142).

Sobchack's arguments are convincing in that if we begin our research by invoking assumed categories like race and sexuality, we are likely to repeat their already assumed significance. Traveling too far down this road results in the essentialization of these categories. On the other hand, failing to invoke them virtually ensures that the categories and their content will be replicated tacitly. If we fail to pay attention to race and sexuality, the accepted and "natural" understanding of these categories as already carried in the dominant culture will be replicated—their racist and homophobic content will be perpetuated. Invoking racial and sexual categories is therefore necessary, but the assumed content of the categories as lived and experience in the concrete lives of persons must be called into question immediately.

Just as the concepts of phenomenology cannot encapsulate the content of the experience of oppression or transformation, it is also true that any given experience of freedom exerted against or the transformation of oppression does not necessarily contain the means or process required for other persons or groups to create a liberating transformation out of the grips of oppression. It is very difficult, in other words, to make *judgments* about when the process and content engaged by somebody or some group results in a successful liberation struggle at the level of the lived body and can therefore suffice as a standard for liberation struggles generally. It is the case, for example, that the critical stance that declares a culture as fundamentally racist or homophobic can become a rigid invocation applied equally (blindly) to all circumstances and thus is capable of enacting its own oppressive gesture. Different people will internalize different aspects of the same racist and homophobic culture. Their strategies for countering that racism and homophobia will necessarily be different. Even when it is the case that I have come to see and know the inherent racism exacted by the dominant culture at the level of my lived body, it is still possible that I might deny the ambiguous and excessive materiality of the lived body of others—I may insist that my lived body is capable of substituting for their body and thus demand that they fit into my understanding of the world and achieve liberation my way. Description requires critique, and critique requires description.

My work in chapter two, for example, has been an essential part of my own struggle to come to terms with the many conflicting messages of my social and existential worlds. For some readers, the stories I offer will resonate strongly with their own experiences. For some, my stories create points of connection through which they can reflect on their own experience and interrogate the specific circumstances in their lives that have led them to their own consciousness of self, other, and world. For others, my stories will seem arcane and distant and will provide very little in the way of movement toward transformative self-consciousness. In a similar way, some may find autobiographical writing to be a very useful activity in struggling against various kinds of oppression. For others, autobiographical writing may be of little importance in that struggle. Nor can one make a judgment about the effectiveness of a liberation struggle based on assumptions about writing style. A text that reads to me as a very abstract and distant academic text could very well be for the author of that work a successful struggle against oppression at the level at the lived body. It is equally true that just because a text is full of autobiographical detail and sensitive self-reflection does not mean that it necessarily adds up to a successful struggle against oppression for either the reader or the writer.[8] There are, in short, many ways to struggle successfully against oppression. To fail to recognize that fact is to in some measure perpetuate oppression.

This line of thinking, however, can lead to the conclusion that because transformations in consciousness are actualized at the level of the person (lived body) and because it is difficult to specify one standard against which one can measure the success of one's struggle against oppression, liberation is simply a matter of each person's journey through her or his own life world. Such a conclusion becomes the ultimate justification for the status quo and denies the fact that each person's account of her or his lived experience is never just hers or his alone but is always also located at a particular point in time and space and the social and discursive dynamics carried therein. Moreover, these suprapersonal dynamics always function to privilege certain histories—particularly when it comes to issues of race and ethnicity—and thus make certain kinds of transformations in consciousness less likely than others. There are always social, discursive, historical, and political reasons why different kinds of ethnic, racial, and sexual identities take the general direction and shapes they do. That is why a purely descriptive phenomenology—a phenomenology that fails to incorporate a critical and historical element in its methodological priorities, that is not also a phenomenology of phenomenology—can be apolitical, can serve the interests of the status quo, and can ultimately become unaccountable to the very connection between lived experience and the social and discursive world by which that experience comes to take the shape it does. This suggests, then, that even the most "purely" descriptive phenomenology is always already critical and interpretive by virtue of the social, discursive, historical, and cultural discriminations carried intersubjectively in praxis. Social, political, and existential issues are always tied to time and place and thus get taken up in a philosophical or applied phenomenology even if the effort explicitly avoids these issues. That Sartre considered the situation of the Jew and the anti-Semite is an obvious example of the social, political, and existential issues that are tied to time and place—there is little likelihood that such a text would have been written prior to Hitler's effort to massacre the Jews. It took Frantz Fanon, however, to use the philosophical and phenomenological effort to explicate the lived experience of persons of color in a racist world. It took Simone de Beauvoir to do the same for women. And, it is important to note in their work (but very few others of their time) that both Fanon and de Beauvoir took up the intersections of race, gender, sexuality, and class. In more contemporary times, it has been the work of lesbians (and queers) of color that has most fully aimed at taking account of the complex interrelations among race, gender, sexuality, and class in a historically specific and situated context. Whatever our position in a particular time and space in the ongoing movement of history, a commitment to interrogating the very parameters by which what we are able to say what we say, think what we think, feel what we feel, and do as we do reduces our risk of simply replicating various kinds of discrimination and exclusions in our very effort to transform them. Ultimately, a taking account is necessary at the level of the lived body—its location in a social, discursive, and historical world and the fleshly and material meanings that are both the means and the results of our particular human situation. It is an effort that is always already critical, interpretive, and phenomenological. In my effort in chapter two to describe the features of my lived experience of coming to consciousness as a lesbian and a Chicana, I deliberately avoided invoking an explicitly critical stance (although that critical stance made the descriptions possible). My next effort, then, is to revisit those descriptions so as to explicate the critical judgments already bound in those descriptions.

SEXUAL AND ETHNIC REVERSALS: THE NECESSARY CROSSING

The relationship between a person's racial and sexual identification is no doubt a very complex and interrelated one. Most white heterosexual people in the contemporary U.S. American culture, I imagine, find it difficult to describe their racial and sexual identifications because they simply take them for granted. Taking racial and sexual identifications for granted makes any critical or critically interpretive description or analysis unlikely. Yet, given a critically interpretive example concerning taken-for-granted notions about sexuality and race, a person might immediately recall and be able to describe many experiences that are themselves critical and interpretive as descriptions.[9]

There is an important and useful tension between the descriptive, critical, and interpretive effort. Each of these efforts always entails the others, yet separating them out for sake of analysis is often useful. In my own effort to phenomenologically interrogate the very conditions by and through which I have come to consciousness as a Chicana, for example, I deliberately bracketed out a critical and interpretive effort so as to focus strongly on the descriptive effort. Yet I would not have been able to engage that descriptive effort except for having already taken up the critical and interpretive ones. This predicament of engaging a purely descriptive effort avoids being naive by also taking account of social, discursive, and political significance of that descriptive effort. At some point, however, the separation of the descriptive from the critical and interpretive creates something capable of distorting the holistic nature of our intersubjective and intrasubjective existence. Perhaps one should acknowledge a certain degree to which all efforts to "get at" the experience of the lived body (whether by description, criticism, interpretation, or some combination thereof) will always be a distortion by virtue of the temporal and spatial distance the "getting at" necessarily has from that which has been. There is a productive tension in the fact that we are situated in time and space and that every moment lived is just that moment as a recollection (repetition backward) and a repetition (recollection forward).[10] In attempting to sort through and describe this complex of recollection and repetition, one is necessarily compelled to create parts of the whole and to look for wholes from the parts. There is a productive tension here as well, provided that the part is not assumed to stand for the whole and that the whole is not assumed to be without the presence of its many parts.

The similarities and differences among my own experience and those of other Chicana lesbians, other lesbians of color, other women of color, other people of color, and others generally have social, discursive, and political significance. The choices I make to single out aspects of my experience for description, criticism, and interpretation also have social, discursive, and political significance. Recognizing these facts, I have been particularly attentive to marking the political issues at stake in foregrounding my experience or advocating a liberation theory that does not have the capacity to interrogate the conditions of its own analysis—that cannot, in other words, account for the limitations entailed within the theory's construction itself. My effort to articulate how my life experience allows me to enter into Chicana feminist work has been informed by a concern for descriptive specificity and a belief that such specificity is necessary in order to form genuine alliances within the very diverse Chicano/ Hispanic community and across ethnic and racial communities of all sorts.

In accounting for the movements of my conscious experience through various stages of ethnic identification in chapter two, I deliberately separated my developing sexual identifications from my developing ethnic identifications. I did this because it seemed to me that the way in which I came to consciousness of each of these parts was distinct. I have been able to identify a specific moment in time, for example, when I experienced an explosion of certainty whereby I knew that my sexual desire directed me strongly toward women. There was no such all-encompassing moment of certainty with regard to my ethnic identity—my ethnic identification was filled with ambiguities. Thus, I was able to proclaim to the world that I was a lesbian even while I was very cautious about making any public claim about my Chicana identification. Separating sexuality and ethnicity in my descriptions allowed me to enter into a Chicana lesbian world while thinking critically about the class and linguistic privileges that my Chicana identifications contained. At the same time, however, my absolute certainty about my sexuality allowed me to take my class, linguistic, and other factors of my situation as a lesbian for granted— I was able to naturalize my lesbianism as a transcendental essence of my being.

In both cases—in considering my lesbian and my Chicana identifications—I retained an inward-outward descriptive orientation toward my descriptions of coming to consciousness. In both cases I reflected carefully on my private experiences and the extent to which I was able to make those private experiences visible in my communicative expression with others and the world—in short, I considered my subjectivity my own (yet I took up this intrasubjectively descriptive effort only after having engaged a critical and interpretive reflection on my life history and circumstance). By virtue of these descriptions of developing subjectivity, I discovered important commonalities with other Chicanas and Chicana lesbians. I discovered subjectivity as intersubjectivity. In neither case, however, did I fully consider the reverse relationship—the relationship between the outside (cultural) notions of what is possible and how they influenced those private experiences I carried within myself. I failed to consider intersubjectivity as subjectivity. This is particularly ironic (although not inappropriate) since I used Sedgwick's (1990) notion of *unknowing-knowing,* by which she specifically identifies, for example, the epistemological space of the closet as being as much as or more a space of the other (to whom one may or may not be out) and culture than it is a space of the person who recognizes her- or himself as lesbian or gay. Sedgwick's terms concern the social and intersubjective spaces of available sexualities (and thus homophobia) as much as or more than the individual consciousness of the person who comes out as gay or lesbian. The fact that my lesbian desire crystallized in absolute clarity in one moment in time whereas my Chicana identification had no such aspect led me to naturalize my lesbian identification and problematize my Chicana identification.

Yet, as I worked through the many revisions of chapter two, I recognized a certain reversal. I began to see ways in which the certitudes that I attributed to my sexual identification came to show great degrees of ambiguity, while the ambiguity I assigned to my ethnic identity came to show great degrees of certitude. The reversal came in the recognition of the social and cultural context that set general parameters within which I came to consciousness both as a Chicana and as a lesbian. The reversal is more than a simple one. A simple reversal in the descriptive analysis provided in chapter two would retain the ethnic-lesbian split and make my ethnic identification into a naturalized and transcendental essence and my lesbian identification into a site of ambiguity. The more significant and revealing reversal lies in the relationship between person and culture, perception and expression, experience and consciousness. To engage these reversals requires that we abandon all notions of naturalized or transcendental essence—which is not the same as saying that we abandon the certainty a person (lived body) experiences in her lived world—and look to sites of ambiguity for more revealing descriptions. In other words, "essences" must be "put back into existence" (Merleau-Ponty 1981, vii; Schrag 1986, 50), where our effort to describe essences of lived experience "exhibits an accentuated critical turn," where they are "means rather than ends" (Schrag 1986, 50; Merleau-Ponty 1981, xiv–xv). It is important to point out, however, that not all descriptions of experience or senses of certainty emerging from ambiguity are equally revealing of the intersubjective worlds from which persons experience their own subjectivity. Thus, we cannot escape the necessity of a *critical* orientation even in our most basic descriptive analyses of lived experience. In short, any final or definitive statement about the subjectivity of intersubjectivity or the intersubjectivity of subjectivity is not possible. Or, in Merleau-Ponty's terms, we must recognize the "impossibility of a complete reduction" (1981, xiv).

My orientation toward my Chicana identity has always been critically orientated. That the critical impulse toward my Chicana identification occurs on the very level of its formation is what makes it a borderland consciousness, a *conciencia de la mestiza*. Reflection on my identification with the Chicana designator did not itself bring a critical impulse but, rather, was *plagued* by critical impulse, a disbelief in the midst of knowing. In the very movement of intentionality, ethnic identification makes of itself an object of perception *because* it is already in question. This process of grappling with identification takes place preconsciously in and on the lived body and is distinct from a distanced application of an assumed criteria of critical significance. Yet, in order for the preconscious struggle of border to become conscious, a certain distance or distanciation is required (Schrag 1986, 48–71). What is the difference between a distanciation that gains access to the border and can therefore make of it a rupture, and a distanciation that keeps the border in place and impassible? There is no question that different people invoking the same criteria of critical judgment—say homophobia—can encounter radically different borders and have radically different possibilities for creating a rupture that makes the border passable. I have often had the experience, for example, of speaking out publicly on issues of homophobia and racism— rarely do I speak of one without speaking of the other. Yet I have had white gay men and lesbians approach me afterward and thank me for speaking out on homophobia, without ever mentioning anything about race or racism. Understandably, they connect with the issue of homophobia and feel it as directly relevant to their own lives and at the level at their lived bodies. I suspect that the failure to mention anything about race or racism stems from the fact that these issues simply do not speak to their lives and their bodies. Issues of race and racism, if taken up, are therefore taken up from a distance that is incapable of rupturing racialized borders. For gay men and lesbians of color, however, the critical consciousness that makes homophobia and racism available as lived experience means that the distance carried in the critical description is capable of creating a rupture that makes crossing the border possible. This is one reason why Anzaldúa argues that queers of color are "supreme crossers." Yet, even still, just because one is a queer of color does not necessarily mean that she or he engages a *conciencia de la mestiza* or is capable of crossing the borders that situate her or him socially, discursively, or historically.

Thus, our task is not one of listing through the oppressive categories we struggle through and "ranking oppressions" (Moraga 1981, 29) but rather one of detailing the very moments in time and place where we confront the borders that define our existence and interrogate their very presence in the preconsciousness that is our lived body's manifestation of our intersubjective coming to subjectivity. In detailing those moments in time and place, moreover, we recognize the essential and contingent status of every descriptive, critical, and interpretive criteria of judgment. There is a danger, for example, of taking the content of my experience as exemplar. The content of my experience provides me with an essential entrée into the very conditions by which I come to think, feel, speak, and act as I do. For some people, my experience will resonate strongly with their own. For others, it will not. But regardless of how the content of experience may or may not resonate with any other person, the process of interrogating that experience, of discovering the very borderland existences that direct our very coming to consciousness of experience, can be considered exemplar. By making the content of my experience explicit, I offer the reader the opportunity to judge for her- or himself the adequacy of the analysis here and, more important, its capacity to speak to their own lives and lived experience. There is one factor, however, that must be noted—and that is the factor of the histories carried within any given border. *La conciencia de la mestiza* is a mestiza consciousness precisely because of the historical and geographical borders from which it emerges. Other borderland consciousnesses, emerging from different geographical and historical borders, may still enact the borderland consciousness described by Anzaldúa. Simply identifying a consciousness as a borderland consciousness is, however, insufficient. Having identified a borderland, we are obliged to detail the personal, social, historical, and discursive recollections and repetitions by which that borderland exists.

NOTES

1. Thank you to Jeffrey Paris for his own work on this point (unpublished manuscript).

2. In fairness, however, one must point out that failure of dominant (white) U.S. feminism to recognize the significance and accomplishments of U.S. women of color is a small example of a self-serving exclusion exacted by a dominant group at the expense of a marginalized or Othered group. See Goldberg (1993) for a discussion of the magnitude of racist exclusions from the modern through the postmodern era.

3. See Ana Castillo (1994, 23–30) for a similar discussion of the conflicting internal discussions of the Chicana as she encounters selves and others both alike and unlike.

4. See Mercer (1993) for a good example as to what gets left out if one takes only the counterstance against the dominant culture. In this remarkable essay, Mercer both engages a blistering critique of the white male photographer's gaze that enacts a colonialist gesture against the black male body and recognizes his own desire for the images of black male body captured by the white male photographer.

5. Anzaldúa uses the term *subconscious* to describe the level at which this inner war takes place. Rather than the spatializing *sub* prefix for consciousness, I prefer to use the temporalizing *pre* conscious because it more clearly suggests the possibility of the contents of the preconscious becoming conscious. Anzaldúa's use of the term suggests that the subconscious does make its way into one's conscious experience.

6. See Gordon (1997, 73–88) for discussion of a racial and sexual matrix whereby racism is necessarily misogynist and homophobic.

7. See also Lanigan (1988, 3–17).

8. Compare Rodriguez (1982).

9. See Castillo (1994, 121–143) and Cisneros (1998, 78–86) for good examples of critical-interpretive descriptions of race and sexuality as lived.

10. See Schrag (1986, 65).

CHICANA FEMINISM AND STRUGGLE IN THE FLESH: RACIST ASSIMILATION AND CULTURAL RECOVERY

I write with the same knowledge, the same sadness, recognizing the full impact of the colonial "experiment" on the lives of Chicanos, mestizos, and Native Americans. Our codices—dead leaves unwritten—lie smoldering in the ashes of disregard, censure, and erasure. *The Last Generation* emerges from those ashes. I write it against time, out of a sense of urgency that Chicanos are a disappearing tribe, out of a sense of this disappearance in my own familia.

—Cherríe Moraga

As long as the majority of mestizos/mestizas refuse to acknowledge the face and heart of the Indian man or woman inside themselves (again, *not to the exclusion* of the other aspects of their being and cultural heritage), they will not be able to realize themselves as complete human beings, in the sense of knowing their own origins, much less give value to the indigenous peoples of the Americas or to the other autochthonous peoples of the world . . . a grave and sad situation for humanity, and for all so-called progressive movements today which mestizos/mestizas are involved in.

—Inéz Hernández-Ávila

The work of contemporary Chicana writers, activists, and academics is an easily ignored part of the people, histories, and cultures that make up the mainstream of late twentieth-century U.S. America. In describing her own work, the Chicana lesbian poet, essayist, and activist Cherríe Moraga (1993) remarks that it "reflects a minor Mexican moment in an otherwise indifferent world literary history" (1). In contrast, Moraga notes, the arrival of Spanish imperialists in the early sixteenth century "was an event of catastrophic consequence to the world." As Anzaldúa (1987) observes, "[T]here were twenty-five million" native people living on the land that is today Mexico and the Yucatán. The Spanish conquest of this land took the lives of more than two-thirds of them. "By 1650," Anzaldúa continues, "only one-and-a-half-million pure-blooded Indians remained" (5). We understand why Todorov (1992) calls the conquest the "greatest genocide in human history" (5). The mestizo race was born of European cultural oppression against the native people and cultures of the Americas. Taking account of our own place at this point in history and seeking to counteract the genocidal legacy and oppressive practices still present is an important part of the very effort taken up by Chicana writers, activists, and academics today. It is an effort we share with Native Americans and our sisters and brothers of all hues and ancestries who come to fight against the dominating and colonialist practices that have characterized the conquest and history of the Americas for more than 500 years.

The colonialist effort in the "new world" involved an explicit use of violence that included, but was not limited to, outright massacre, the introduction and deliberate spread of disease, enslavement, and rape. Within this context of violence, some of the Spanish colonialists, such as Bartolomé de Las Casas, advocated a milder approach centering on the conversion of the native people and their cultures to Christianity. Even still, Las Casas's (1992) passionate defense of the Indians against Sepúlveda's justifications for their annihilation in point of fact did very little to stem the flow of violence and destruction thrust on them. Whether explicit uses of violence were advocated or not, the assimilationist effort remained a constant force directed on the native people encountered by the colonialists. Not only were the native people subjected to physical violence of all sorts, they were equally subjected to sustained attacks on their social and cultural way of life.

Because this assimilation effort is directed toward the darker racialized Other so as to serve the economic, social, and political interests of the dominating culture, the assimilationist effort is always already a *racist* effort.[1] Moreover, because the colonialist and assimilationist effort is an expression of the colonizing culture's already-held perception of their superiority over the darker racialized Other, no matter how faithfully the darker racialized Other assimilates into the dominant culture, the dominant culture will always assign an inferior status to her or him—the darker and more racializable a person is, the less likely she or he will ever escape the social double bind created and sustained by and within the racist-assimilationist culture itself.[2] The notion of the "melting pot" is thus revealed as a "bleaching pot" (Moraga 1981), where one must "renounce—often in clearly public ways—one's subjectivity," who one is by name, by culture "and as far as possible, in color" (Goldberg 1993, 219). Under racist assimilation the darker racialized Others are encouraged to believe that by embracing the whole of "American values" they will be accorded equal status within a country where "all men are created equal." Yet race-based knowledge persists at the level of cultural perception, so that to the degree that one is easily marked (by skin color, language capacity, sexuality, class, and so on), one is "overdetermined from the outside." Being overdetermined from the outside means that the racially marked Other remains anonymous (Fanon 1967; Goldberg 1993, 210) and thus has very little hope of being actually recognized as "American" even if one does, indeed, embrace the whole of "American values." Whereas individual subjectivity is accorded to the unmarked person and allows for the individuality of "Americans" to be expressed and perceived, the racially marked person remains locked into a racist-signifying system whereby the darkness of skin color dominates all other possible perceptions and thus the ideology of individuality carried in U.S. American culture is withheld.

The work of many contemporary Chicana scholars seeks to understand the place of Chicanas across generations of racist-assimilationist culture and engages liberatory efforts to counteract the erasures produced by it. In taking up this effort, many Chicana scholars confront simultaneously issues of racism, sexism, and homophobia as obstacles that when left unchecked work against the very liberatory efforts taken. In countering racist assimilation and the effects of sexism and homophobia, many Chicana scholars recognize that going back is impossible because the past can never be what it was again and therefore confront the question as to how one goes forward after the fact of cultural and historical loss. This is a particularly relevant point for my own work. Other Chicana scholars, situated differently within the erasures of culture and history, will, no doubt, have different pasts that are more and less available than my own. Yet there is a certain degree to which all of us, Chicana, Native American, and African diaspora, must consider the question of an irrecoverable history and cultural heritage. What does it mean to recover a cultural heritage when important aspects of the cultural heritage could be irrecoverable? Asking such a question guards against the falsely liberatory effort involved in an idealistic or romanticized return to a past that can never be again. At the same time, however, traces of those erasures remain. The racist-assimilationist effort has *not* reached its logical outcome. Black, brown, and native people remain on this land, and our cultural heritages are present and active despite being difficult to see when looked for through the eyes of racist U.S. American culture. Native American culture remains present on this land despite more than five centuries of domination (Allen 1992). Mestizo ancestry, itself a hybrid offspring of those five centuries of domination, is not a fully assimilated cultural identity (Hernández-Ávila 1997).

Chicana studies is an interdisciplinary field that features work in disciplines all across the humanities and social sciences. Yet I think it is fair to say that there is a certain degree to which all of us working under the Chicana studies sign seek to counteract the racist, classist, and sexist erasures produced by the dominant U.S. American culture. Such a description cannot be said to adequately characterize all of Chicana studies, but activism and advocacy in the interest of Chicanas, our families, and our communities are certainly driving forces for much contemporary Chicana scholarship. Given the particularities of my own life and entrance into Chicana studies, I am particularly concerned with the potentialities of recovering that which has been lost. By interrogating the effects of racist-assimilationist culture across generations, I am seeking a recovery that features process over content. Because Mexican Americans are a widely diverse group, each of us will have had different experiences that we connect to the fact of our Mexican American ancestry. Rather than compare experiences so as to determine which ones are more or less "Mexican American," "Chicana," or "Chicano," we would do better to interrogate the conditions and processes through which we have come to have the experiences we have. My own life experiences lead me to emphasize process over content precisely because racist-assimilationist culture has worked a certain effect on my own family history. In featuring process over content it becomes possible to make connections across a wide range of differing experiences of race, ethnicity, class, and sexuality. Potentialities for alliances across these many categories emerge not because the content of our experience is the same but because we recognize a common enemy in the racist-sexist-classist-homophobic-assimilationist culture we share. In this way, our activism and advocacy can cohere around antiracist, antisexist, anticlassist, antihomophobic, and antiassimilationist practices despite our widely varying experiences. Rather than compare experience so as to judge who can count as this or that, our experiences become the site of interrogation whereby we may come to better understand how a racist-sexist-classist-homophobic-assimilationist culture works so as to more effectively counteract it.

The particularities of my own life, especially those centering on my coming to consciousness as a Chicana and a lesbian, have forced certain borders into the fabric of my very lived experience. These borders are characterized by ambiguity and an unknowingness that makes any fixing of those borders difficult. To assign a content to one side of these borders and a different content to the other side of them has not been possible. Instead, I have been left with sorting through and picking out particular features, only to find a certain arbitrariness to any one feature selected for reflective attention. Despite the apparent futility of not being able to fix the borders and their respective contents, the ambiguity and apparent arbitrariness gives way to a certain potentiality of process. My own Chicana feminist effort takes up the challenge of engaging a nonstationary critical consciousness that seeks a cultural recovery that is necessarily antiracist, antisexist, and antihomophobic and is capable of interrogating the conditions of its own practice. In overcoming the fact of cultural loss without succumbing to lies and false histories presented by the racist-assimilationist, sexist, homophobic, and classist culture, many Chicana writers, activists, and academics embrace their own borderland consciousness as lived on and through their bodies; engage a recursively critical orientation toward the historical, geographical, and social borders they cross; and offer new possibilities for understanding the many differences and divides that often creates multileveled struggles within our own conscious experience and in our relationships with others. It is an engagement with self and other that constitutes a transformative and liberatory practice aimed at the very point of possibility of actualization—it is a point of communication and transformation in praxis. A brief examination of the development of contemporary Chicana feminism provides a basis from which we may articulate the specifics of the cultural, social, and personal contexts in which such communicative and transformative praxis may be engaged.

THE DEVELOPMENT OF CONTEMPORARY CHICANA FEMINISM

The development of contemporary Chicana scholarship illustrates a transformative potential in two distinct but related ways. In one sense, Chicana scholarship provides new accounts of history and culture that bring to light the common experiences and sociopolitical struggles of native women during the Spanish conquest, of Mexicanas during the Euro-American encroachment onto the land of what is today the southwestern United States, and of contemporary women of Mexican American descent. In this way, Chicana scholarship challenges the very discursive terms through which we normatively understand Native American and Mexican American history and culture. In a second and related sense, contemporary Chicana feminism creates new interpretive and critical frames through which Chicanas can reread history and critically reinterpret the meaningfulness of their own lived experience.

The body of intellectual, artistic, and critical work we know today as Chicana feminism has its most obvious roots in the social upheavals experienced by a generation of Mexican American women during the 1960s and 1970s (García 1989). It was a decidedly U.S. American movement that shares important points of convergence with the other great political movements of the time: the black power movement, the American Indian movement, the anti-Vietnam movement, and the second wave of the women's rights movement.[3] Fighting across front lines in states all throughout the western and southwestern United States, *El Movimiento* (as the Chicano movement came to be known) addressed a variety of social, political, economic, and educational concerns. Leaders such as Cesar Chavez and

Dolores Huerta, Rodolfo "Corky" Gonzales, and José Angel Gutiérrez led the United Farm Workers movement in California, organized communities and advocated for political self-determination in Colorado, and established the Raza Unida Party in Texas (García 1997). Self-declared Chicanos and Chicanas radically challenged the primary and secondary educational system for the erasures of Mexican American history and the racist ways in which education was delivered. By using boycotts, organizing participation in the political processes, confronting racist educational systems, and using the pen and the brush in artistic expression, the Chicano movement of the 1960s and 1970s marks one of the most important moments of a group-based activism and community self-empowerment in U.S. American history.

Yet, as Alma García (1997) points out, there was also something fundamentally paradoxical about *El Movimiento*. A call for equal rights and opportunities under the law and within the social world, *El Movimiento* was also a nationalist ethnic separatist effort (García 1997, 2). There is good reason to embrace nationalism as a strategy against the negative effects of a racist culture that denies the legitimacy and significance of Mexican American cultural heritage. In this regard, we should understand "racist" in the terms offered by Goldberg (1993, 8) as a pernicious and transforming set of concepts—that is, racisms—which are bound to "the terms of and sustained by an underlying culture" or signifying system; U.S. American culture is itself a racist culture, founded and sustained on principles that have supported a long and complex history of legally authorized and/or socially accepted racist practices. The flexibility of these signifying systems of culture allows various conceptualizations of race to function as exclusion across a wide variety of discursive contexts. Within the context of modern liberalism, we have a "racializing paradox" that is displayed in the fact that "*liberalism's commitment to principles of universality is practically sustained only by the reinvented and rationalized exclusions of racial particularity*" (Goldberg 1993, 39 [emphasis added]). The very call for "equality" is intelligible only on the basis of the racist, sexist, homophobic, and capitalist discriminations of U.S. American society that give rise to race-based inequalities in the first place. Because the social, economic, and legal discourses of contemporary U.S. American culture are founded on these liberal principles, the call for a nationalist ethnic separatist movement and a collective ethnic consciousness based in a fundamental critique of the dominant culture is *necessary* to offset the racist norms of U.S. American culture.

El Movimiento's call for a collective ethnic and nationalist separatist consciousness came to be known as *Chicanismo,* and it "emphasized cultural pride as a source of political unity and strength capable of mobilizing Chicanos and Chicanas into an oppositional political group within the dominant political landscape in the United States" (García 1997, 3). There is an inherent paradox in pursuing an oppositional politics while appealing to the value of equality within the U.S. American systems of justice and opportunity. On the one hand, Chicanismo provided a powerful source of cultural pride that became an important motivator for the thousands of Chicano and Chicana activists working on many fronts within the U.S. American social, political, economic, and educational landscape. It also became a precursor to an outpouring of Chicano artistic expression. Chicanas made crucial contributions to every aspect of this overall movement yet experienced their own paradoxical situation within Chicanismo: To the extent that Chicano nationalism embraced, justified, and perpetuated sexist norms, Chicanas found their contributions trivialized, subordinated, and often ignored. Thus, Chicanas recognized the need to move against racism and sexism simultaneously. Chicanas' recognition of their paradoxical situation within Chicanismo formed the basis for the development of what we have come to know today as Chicana feminism.

As primarily working-class Chicanas, these early movement activists were "acutely aware of the discrimination they faced" and agitated for change relative to the specific kinds of racial and sexist discrimination they faced across a broad spectrum of issues that included "welfare rights, child care, health, birth control, sterilization, legal rights, prison experience of Chicanas, sex roles, images of Chicanas, heroines of history, labor struggles" (Córdova 1994, 78). For Chicanas fighting in these social, economic, and political battles, experiences of male domination within the Chicano movement led to the development of a Chicana feminist consciousness that "viewed the struggle against sexism within the Chicano movement and the struggle against racism in the larger society as central ideological components" of their activist efforts (García 1997, 5). Many of these Chicanas, having worked in *El Movimiento* during the 1960s, came by the early 1970s to seriously question some of the core values of the Chicano movement itself. Most prominent among these core values was the glorification and romanticization of the Chicano family and women's role within it. They identified the influence of the Catholic Church as a major source of the patriarchal sexism that suffused Chicanismo and reached back through generations to courageous Mexican and Mexican American women who defied the passive-female norm carried in the call for a collective ethnic consciousness. These foremothers of contemporary Chicana feminism "understood that one of their first needs as activists was to become an integral part of the movement as leaders, as conference speakers and not as 'decorations'" (Córdova 1994, 177). In this way and others, the Chicana feministas of the early 1970s courageously took on the difficult task of challenging "the essentialism of the movement" while simultaneously standing firm within their own cultural boundaries and in opposition to the dominant culture (García 1997, 18). As the early 1970s progressed into the mid- and later 1970s, Chicanas began more and more to turn their activist attention directly to the development of a specifically Chicana feminist consciousness that demanded their own space within the Chicano movement.

One of the major obstacles faced by Chicana feminist activists during the 1970s was the accusation that their call for a feminist consciousness was a betrayal of Chicano culture and an untenable collusion with white feminism and thus Anglo culture. Yet the specificity of Chicana feminists' advocacy challenges this notion. By virtue of these early Chicana feministas' work, both in their communities and in *El Movimiento*, they came to know that a genuine struggle for liberation must address oppression in every form in which it is encountered. The nationalist discourse that informed *El Movimiento* perpetuated a strict binary distinction of cultural-loyalist versus assimilationist-traitor. This strict binary functioned exclusively, so that one proved one's loyalty by embracing Chicano culture in its taken-for-grantedness within the community. Any gravitation toward Anglo culture became evidence of betrayal to the movement. By virtue of their effort to fight sexist norms within the nationalist discourse of *El Movimiento*, Chicanas discovered the point at which the nationalist discourse itself was not capable of critical self-interrogation. Chicanas who critiqued the gender bias within their own movement were perceived to be selling out the interests of the Chicano movement to the interests of the women's movement. The dominance of the nationalist discourse in the early 1970s thus made invisible the fact that these Chicana activists "had very well developed notions of what [their own] needs were and were very clear that they were distinct from those of Anglo feminists" (Córdova 1994, 177). Chicanas had both the ideology of the Chicano movement and the consciousness of their lived experiences as a basis to understand "their oppression and their relation to Chicano men in a historical political economic context" (Córdova 1994, 177). A danger encountered in all liberation struggles is the tendency to assert that one knows what is unknown (as described in chapter two) and therefore what is necessary to learn in order achieve liberation. Many men of *El Movimiento*, like many men who worked with the Black Panthers (Davis 1990), asserted a knowingness that precluded acknowledging what was unknown to them—namely, the ways in which their own sexist attitudes and beliefs actually hindered a genuine and common struggle with Chicanas for liberation and transformation. There were, however, some men within the movement who acknowledged such an unknowingness and recognized the political importance of taking that unknowingness seriously as a necessary part of liberatory struggle. Consider these words from a Chicano at an early 1980s meeting of the National Association of Chicano Studies:

We can't reduce the question of sexism to something you can quantify, or some kind of model or some kind of simple policy statement. We have to begin to look at where we as men are coming from and what we are feeling and thinking inside of ourselves in regards not only to women but to men also. I see a great deal of resistance to that. I find that most men want to see sexism as a policy decision only and that it is not tied into one's spirit and soul. In terms of men, we have to go back to step one and we have to look at ourselves, and see what is going on inside ourselves and in our relations to people. We have to look at our patterns of thinking and see if we are trying to impose those patterns on some-one else. (cited in Córdova 1994, 185)

I think it is fair to say that much of Chicana feminism has always been a struggle rooted in spirit and soul against racism, sexism, economic discrimi-nation, and the complex interrelations of forces that have perpetuated a whole range of oppressive circumstances in the everyday concrete lives of Chicanas and their communities. Far from being sellouts, these early feministas were the first mestiza border crossers. It was their work that laid the ground for what Anzaldúa would come to call *la conciencia de la mes-tiza* and for the development of the significant body of scholarship con-sidering the theory and methodology entailed therein. In short, these early Chicana feministas are foremothers of some of the most important con-temporary developments in understanding the linkage between the con-ceptual-ideological and practical-lived aspects of liberation struggles.

By the end of the 1970s, Chicana feminists had already established an important body of critical social science, historical, and literary work that critiques the racist and sexist ideologies that have informed and jus-tified the subordination of Native and Mexican American women and men since the first landings of Europeans on the American continents. Córdova (1994) identifies four major points to emerge out of Chicana writing dur-ing the last half of the 1990s:

(1) The Chicana is not inherently passive—nor is she what the stereo-types say she is; (2) She has a history rooted in a legacy of struggle; (3) Her history and her contemporary experiences can only be understood in the context of a race and class analysis; and (4) The Chicana is in the best position to describe and define her own reality. (179–180)

These four points, taken together, form the basis for a Chicana feminist practice that Chela Sandoval comes to call "the theory and method of op-positional consciousness in a postmodern world" (1991), a "methodology of the oppressed" (1995), and "mestizaje as method" (1998). Each of these four points emerging out of Chicana writing emphasizes a consciously engaged struggle taking place within the very lives and on the very bodies of Chicanas themselves. The first point is an inherently critical orientation toward the terms both mainstream and Chicano culture use toward Chicanas. It is a recognition that the Chicana is not circumscribed by the notions of her carried in the dominant and even nondominant social, historical, and cultural worlds—she is more than what a stereotype would have her be. From this critical orientation, Chicana writers can then acknowledge, even foreground, the fact of the struggle taken up in their own lives. This then creates a basis for searching out and recognizing a history of struggle of others who preceded the work of contemporary Chicanas. That struggle is recognized as essentially involving race and class (in addition to the already taken up issues of sex/gender). And finally, by virtue of recognizing and engaging these features and functions of struggle in the fabric of her very life, the Chicana recognizes that she herself is in the best position to speak to her history and circumstance. Simple as these four points may seem, taken together, they recognize the inherent interrelatedness of each individual Chicana's struggle, the fact of history and its representations, and her capacity to intervene in that interrelatedness and thus create different possibilities for her own and others' human becoming in the world. Yet the struggle engaged is never easy and always dangerous. Border crossing requires stepping across to both sides, sides that are incompatible, often in very hostile ways. The clear and simple realization that one is not what the stereotypes say can leave one facing an open space where the possibilities of social and personal becoming remain ambiguous and available for exertions of existential freedom. To step outside the normative categories, to defy the stereotype and question the legitimacy of current understanding, is also to encounter hostility often coming from both sides of the border. There is some sense in which the border crosser finds herself always open for some kind of attack. This concept of border, so important in contemporary Chicana scholarship, is worthy of a lengthy quotation. Anzaldúa (1987) describes the concept this way:

> A border is a dividing line, a narrow strip along a steep edge. A borderland is a vague and undetermined place created by the emotional residue of an unnatural boundary. It is in a constant state of transition. The prohibited and forbidden are its inhabitants. *Los atravesados* live here: the squint-eyed, the perverse, the queer, the troublesome, the mongrel, the mulatto, the half-breed, the half dead; in short, those who cross over, pass over, or go through the confines of the "normal." Gringos in the U.S. Southwest consider the inhabitants of the borderlands transgressors, aliens—whether they possess documents or not, whether they're Chicanos, Indians or Blacks. Do not enter, trespassers will be raped, maimed, strangled, gassed, shot. The only "legitimate" inhabitants are those in power, the whites and those who align themselves with whites. (3–4)

Contemporary Chicana lesbians embrace this "borderland" existence by virtue of a specific kind of recognition. It is consciousness coming to see the complex workings of consciousness itself that is reducible neither to the collective history of a people nor to the individual experiences of one person. It is a recognition that emerges out of a real bodily awareness of damages already done and damages waiting to be done. But out of this recognition of damages done and damages waiting to be done, the borderlands of Chicana consciousness also break free to embrace ever new sets of possibilities for self and community that portend radical transformations in consciousness and culture.

In portending these radical transformations, "borderland" existence makes a politics out of identity and location. Yet this is a kind of political identity and location that does not invoke a single standard or location. It is a kind of political identification that itself is in motion, recognizes the contingent nature of any given political strategy, and therefore requires an open-ended, flexible, and self-reflexive orientation toward the ongoing process of making oneself and the world meaningful. As Goldberg (1993) suggests, "In the final analysis, the only and necessarily contingent guarantee of freedom is the practice of freedom itself, is freely living the conditions of expressive space" (211). The journey from "freely living the conditions of expressive space" to the complex theoretical and political judgments about how people and a culture is or is not successful in creating the general conditions for this expression is crucially important.

ATTENDING TO BORDERLANDS

Attending to our borderlands, our histories, and our worlds necessarily means looking at *la familia*—the very place where the intimacy of cultural legacy is carried. It is easy to speak in grand historical generalizations. It is much more difficult to take the key points of a historical analysis and put it through the sieve of one's own *familia*, both immediate and across generations. *La conciencia de la mestiza* can never be a distanced or generalized theorization about racist assimilation but must involve a self-reflexive engagement with the facticity of our very lives. Throughout this project, I have tried to connect every theorization to the concrete and material realities necessarily lived (on and through the body) as I have moved through the project itself. This effort has made an explicit consideration of *mi familia* necessary and unavoidable. I have come to consider, for example, the fact that my paternal grandmother's life reaches back to the very beginning of the twentieth century, when the situation for Mexican Americans was decidedly different than for those of my generation.[4] The signing of the Treaty of Guadalupe Hidalgo in 1848 is not that far removed from her life and was certainly a very real part of her parents' and grandparents' lives. It is very clear to me that while the temporal distances between me and my great-great-grandparents is really not that far, the psychic and historical distances are tremendous. It is also clear to me that a major reason for those huge psychic and historical distances has exactly to do with the racist-assimilationist forces that define so much of what contemporary U.S. American culture is and has been. The work of Chicana historians, like Vicki Ruiz (1993), Deena González (1993), and many others, helps us bridge these gaps by allowing us to learn about the people and lives that we would not have otherwise and thereby to see the often subtle cultural heritages that have survived the massive onslaught of racist oppression. It then becomes possible—despite the many silences and erasures—to move forward with something to counter the inevitable destruction enacted by a racist-assimilationist, sexist, and homophobic culture. In the following discussion, I engage the work of Chicana historian Vicki Ruiz (1993), who studies the circumstances and experiences of young Mexican American women in southern Texas who "came of age" from the 1920s through the 1950s. I take up this discussion specifically because it speaks directly to the circumstances that my father faced as he was "coming of age" in southern Texas in the 1930s and 1940s. My father, born in 1928 in McAllen, Texas, grew up in this time and place. Although Ruiz focuses on the pressures faced by young Mexican American women during this time, her stories resonate with the stories told to me by my father about his own life growing up. Ruiz's work describes some of the many cultural double binds at work for young Mexican Americans of these decades—double binds that can be identified as emblematic to the whole of time and culture under colonialist domination.

If it is true—and I imagine it is—that the Anglos who migrated west following the signing of the Treaty of Guadalupe Hidalgo in 1848 were motivated to a large degree by the simple and understandable hope of making it rich and building a promising future, then it is probably also true that by the early decades of the twentieth century aspirations for wealth, for moving up the socioeconomic ladder and achieving the American Dream, were deeply entrenched in all those who lived on and immigrated to the land of the United States of America. By the first decades of the twentieth century, the mythology of the American Dream seems to define much of U.S. American culture. For both the Mexicans who immigrated to the United States during this time and for those U.S. citizens of Mexican descent whose history on the land of the United States pre-dates the Treaty of Guadalupe Hidalgo, the dream of "making it big" suffuses all their personal and cultural lives. For those young Mexican Americans growing up from the 1920s to the 1950s in the southwestern United States, the brutalities and dirty dealing of the frontier days seem to have receded into the background of history—a consequence, no doubt, of the racism and ethnocentrism of the Euro-American culture that encourages everyone to believe that all persons are treated equally. In her own study, Ruiz (1993) examines the "forces of Americanization and the extent to which they influenced a generation of Mexican American women coming to age during the 1920s and 1930s" (109).

Throughout her essay, Ruiz (1993) examines "education, employment and media as agents of Americanization" (110). "Americanization," Ruiz asserts, "seemed to seep into the barrios from all directions—from schools, factories, and even [Mexican Americans' own] ethnic press" (113). Education served the function of encouraging Mexican Americans to hope for achieving the American Dream even while systematic discrimination in employment tended to restrict upward mobility. Through education, young Mexican Americans were encouraged to speak only English because Spanish was seen as a "dirty language" associated with poor and backward people.[5] Young men especially were encouraged to take vocational education and adopt life aspirations limited to the working class. During the 1920s and 1930s, young girls were encouraged to take typing classes and become secretaries even though, as Ruiz points out, "few southwestern businesses hired Spanish-surnamed office workers. In 1930, only 2.6 percent of all Mexican women wage earners held clerical jobs" (111). Education was, among other social influences, a place where young Mexican Americans found "contradictions between the promise of the American dream and the reality of restricted mobility and ethnic prejudice" (110). As Ruiz summarizes, "In the abstract, education raised people's expectations, but in practice, particularly for men, it trained them for low-status, low-paying jobs" (121). Even solidly middle-class Mexicans who immigrated to the United States during this time "found themselves subject to ethnic prejudice that did not discriminate by class" (114).

Racism, as Ruiz (1993) points out, was rampant in the lives of Mexican Americans during this time. For example, "between 1931 and 1934, an estimated one third of the Mexican population in the United States (over 500,000 people) were either deported or repatriated to Mexico, even though many were native U.S. citizens" (120). What Ruiz says about the barrios in the Southwest during the first half of the twentieth century rings just as true today: "Both in urban and rural areas, ethnicity became not only a matter of personal choice and heritage but also an ascribed status imposed by external sources" (121). The relationship between this "ascribed status imposed by external sources" and individual person's own sense of self and place is crucially important in bringing to light this "complex reality of cultural accommodation and ongoing resistance" (González

1993, 86) that has characterized every generation since the first landings of the Europeans on the American continents. Considering the tangible presence of both external prejudice and internal aspirations for success in the lives of these young Mexican Americans, Ruiz (1993) suggests that

> it is no surprise that many teenagers developed a shinning idealism as a type of psychological ballast. Some adolescents . . . believed that education was the key to mobility, while others placed their faith in the application of Max Factor's bleaching cream. Whether they struggled to further their education or tried to lighten their skin color, Mexican Americans sought to protect themselves from the damaging effects of prejudice. (121)

One might consider achieving education and applying bleaching cream to one's face to be two drastically different strategies for Mexican Americans to negotiate externally imposed racial judgments with their own internal sense of self and aspirations for a future. In the final analysis, each strategy produced the same effects. The bleaching of one's skin only makes obvious the general pressures exerted within a racist-assimilationist culture. At least with a bleaching cream one can remove it from one's face, one's home, and refuse to purchase such a product anymore. Primary education, on the other hand, is never so controllable by the young person who consumes it. The effects of uncritically believing in education as the key to one's future has a far more damaging and permanent effect on one's ethnic psyche than the application of bleaching cream to one's face ever could.

I remember in my own primary school education during the early 1970s learning about the missions established all along the California coast. Like countless other Mexican Americans of my time, previous times, and even today, I got the message that these missions were good things and that they helped spread religion and education and created opportunities for the people who came to them. I got nothing in that education about the lived struggles of the native and Mexican people of this land to retain their own cultural and personal possessions and certainly nothing to allow me to identify with lifelong struggles of people of my own native and Mexican heritage and the flesh and blood that they have laid all across the land of the southwestern United States. In this way education serves the general cultural effort to erase not only the struggles of Native and Mexican Americans *as Americans* but also the essential role that Native and Mexican Americans have played in the very history of this land. The fact that so many white people born and raised in the southwestern United States know and see utterly nothing of the rich Mexican and Mexican American cultural history that makes it what it is today is yet another sign of a fundamentally racist culture. If racist exclusions were not part and parcel of contemporary U.S. American culture, then it would be commonplace for white U.S. Americans to "be intellectually *and* culturally influenced by the thought of black [and red and brown] people" (Goldberg 1993, 218). Whites and darker others would thereby live within a social momentum where is it ordinary to think through and identify with "the conditions of possibility for being black [or red or brown], indeed, for whites to be black [or red or brown]" (218).

Given the "bleaching" effect of Anglo education, it is easy to understand why, within the psyches of young Mexican Americans during the first half of the twentieth century, we have a generation of people who believed in the American Dream and "that hard work would bring material rewards and social acceptance" (Ruiz 1993, 111). Even while they were "painfully aware of prejudice and discrimination, people of this generation placed faith in themselves and in the system" (122). The mythos of "American" ideology is that it is the land of opportunity, that anyone can become an American, and that hard work will overcome all. As Ruiz summarizes, "The desire to prove oneself appears as a running theme in twentieth century Mexican American history" (122). Without a context to understand the systematic discrimination exacted against Mexican Americans, this belief in oneself, hard work, and the ability to overcome can turn, when success is not achieved, into the internalization of the worst images of Mexican Americans. The moment that those worst images are internalized, self-hatred may begin to take hold. As Ruiz argues,

> the impact of Americanization was most keenly felt at the level of personal aspiration. We felt that if we worked hard, proved ourselves, we could become professional people, asserted Rose Echeverria Mulligan. Braced with such idealism, Mexican Americans faced prejudice, segregation and economic segmentation. Though they considered themselves Americans, other perceived them as less than desirable foreigners. (120)

We have here the makings of a double bind in the life world of young Mexican Americans during this time. Internally embracing aspirations for success in "American" terms, they nonetheless are subject to virulent expressions of negative stereotyping.

But then, what about the Mexican Americans who were successful, those who "made it"? Aspirations for success for young Mexican Americans are defined within the notion of the American Dream, where "success" equals the achievement of wealth and socioeconomic status. Thus, we have the notion of a "successful Mexican American" as one who embodies all the signs of a white middle-class heterosexual American—that is, one who can be understood entirely within the Euro-"American" ideology with all its ethnocentrism and racism. It is precisely this connection between "success" in U.S. American culture, the signs of middle-class standards of living, and presumed assimilation that leads Chicano scholars, among others, to suggest that this "assimilation" constitutes a betrayal to Mexican and Mexican American people and culture. Yet, as Ruiz and other Chicana scholars point out, this may not be the best way to understand what González (1993) calls the "complex reality of cultural accommodation and ongoing resistance" (76). This is, in fact, precisely Ruiz's (1993) point when she describes "[t]he impact of material assimilation" and how

> the purchase of an automobile, a sewing machine, and the other accouterments of U.S. consumer society . . . signaled the realization (or the potential for realizing) the American dream. (122)

While the attainment of these outward signs of "acculturation" are often used as a basis on which judgments of "assimilationist" and therefore "betrayer" have been made, Ruiz suggests that "the ideological impact of material acculturation has been over-rated" (123). In Ruiz's terms, one cannot "equate the desire for material goods with the abandonment of Mexican values" (123).

How, then, are we to understand the complex interworkings of aspirations for success as they collide with one's own knowledge of oneself as a Mexican American? If it is shortsighted to simply "equate the desire for material goods with the abandonment of Mexican values" (Ruiz 1993, 123), then how do we go about understanding this complex interplay of clashing cultural values? If the desire to acquire material goods lacks the power to signify cultural assimilation, then what signs do we look to in seeking to understand this process of "assimilation" into mainstream Euro-American culture?

STRUGGLE IN THE FLESH

Recognizing the insufficiency of the social stereotype to account for who one is opens the way for understanding the *materiality of consciousness in communication with itself.* Prior to such a recognition the social stereotype simply suffuses one's consciousness and creates a material presence on the body and in the world that maintains the stereotype itself. In one case the person might even come to love (narcissistically) that stereotype and thus evade the existential and self-reflexive question as to how it is that one is who one is. In another case the preconscious recognition of the stereotype leads the person to hate her- or himself by virtue of that stereotype—the person then spends a lifetime fighting a losing battle of trying to not be that stereotype while actually believing it to be an accurate assessment of who and how one is. Taking up the self-reflexive questions that come by virtue of the conscious recognition of the inherent inadequacy of any social (anonymous) stereotype to account for who and how one is, however, immediately engages one in the complex movements of consciousness as it negotiates the internal aspirations of a person in the face of an ascribed status externally imposed. Engaging this aspect of the materiality of consciousness precludes any static notion of identity and emphasizes the very motility of consciousness as *phenomenological* intentionality. Pursuing this kind of effort gives us an entirely different sort of "education" than any kind encouraged within the dominant institutions of education. It is an education that takes seriously the presence of persons in the world and the world in persons. It is an education that requires the varying and often radical perspectives and histories of nondominant people but that does not fall into the trap of making any one of those perspectives or histories a final word or ultimate truth about the state of things. Rather, those perspectives and histories must be put into dialectical engagement with the ongoing apprehensions of particular consciousnesses as they are embodied by particular persons in particular times and particular places. And here is where we must emphasize the importance—especially for the racially marked darker others whose histories have been distorted and erased—of looking to our own familial lives, reading them in dialectic with the various histories we are offered today, and moving forward in a radical engagement that refuses any final point or destination as goal. This kind of work is both political and personal.

Throughout this text I have tried to engage just such an effort, and, I have tried to engage it in such a way that no set formula or procedure can be lifted and simply taken to be applied somewhere else. I have tried to feature my own lived experience in such a way that others might find identification with aspects of that experience and be encouraged therefore to take up a similar effort within their own lives. Yet this work is much more than an autobiographical account that seeks to make identification with others with similar lives. It is also a sustained study and application of a communicative praxis informed by semiotic phenomenology (Lanigan 1988, 1991, 1992). Throughout this project I have resisted describing a research methodology, although I have embraced a methodological procedure of description, reduction, and interpretation in this work. There is a reason why semiotics and phenomenology should always be both a philosophy and a research procedure, and it is because we can never escape the fact of our own human presence in that which we perceive and express. To take up a philosophy or a research procedure without reflection on the very ways in which we ourselves are present in the philosophical and research effort is to evade the most irreducible fact of our human existence—namely, that we speak, feel, think, and do. There is a concrete materiality in the very fact of our existence. To take that for granted is to succumb to whatever momentum of the social, historical, and discursive world are present, no matter how violent and humanly degrading that momentum may be.

My focus on Chicana feminism has been necessary because the history of my Mexican and Native American ancestors has been most violently attacked. The fact that I am a Chicana and a lesbian, an academic, a daughter, a granddaughter, a sister, a friend, and so on has everything to do with the possibilities of this work emerging as it has. Of all the things that I "am" being, a Chicana and a lesbian has been problematic within the given understanding of the dominant U.S. American culture. It has therefore been from the perspective as a Chicana lesbian that I have had the most ground to travel relative to the features and functions of the social, discursive, and historical worlds within which I exist. Recognizing the racist exclusions perpetuated by the dominant culture provides a critical basis from which it is possible to resignify events previously experienced and create new possibilities for social becoming. Antiracist, antisexist, and antihomophobic efforts take up precisely this effort. But it can never be an effort of anticipated ends. Ultimately, these efforts must be lived on and through the lived body, the social body, the historical body, the body politic. It requires a commitment to communication and transformation in the very praxis by which we have come to experience what we experience, think what we think, feel what we feel, and do what we do. This project is a taking up of precisely that effort.

NOTES

1. See Castañeda (1993, 15–33) for an excellent discussion of violently racist and sexist practices authorized by the Spanish Viceroy Bucareli, implemented by the padres running missions in Alta California, and aimed at assimilating Native American women and men.

2. In his discussion of assimilation, Goldberg (1993) notes that prior to the establishment of the legal and political means to address the specifically black-racist exclusions of U.S. American culture, assimilation into the U.S. American mainstream did not apply to black Americans because "they were deemed inherently unassimilable" (219).

3. The irony of this statement must be noted. All of these great political movements of U.S. American history are decidedly born of U.S. American culture. This despite the fact that the very movements themselves were necessitated by the tacitly accepted cultural view that the interests represented by these movements were somehow un-American.

4. See Orozco (1999, 106–120) for an excellent consideration of cultural heritage as it is lived across generations.

5. See Mendoza-Denton (1999, 39–56) for an excellent discussion of how attitudes and policies toward Spanish-speaking students continue to decrease their opportunities for success in primary education and access to secondary education.

6

CHICANA Y CHICANA: A DIALOGUE ON RACE, CLASS, AND CHICANA IDENTITY

There is a certain sense in which all the work accomplished thus far is already a dusty artifact of the lived struggle that produced it. Writing, it seems, is somehow insufficient in itself for the effort taken up here. It seems as though we need to engage in the immediacy of speaking and listening so as to be moved, to gain access to self via others. For this reason, among others, I conclude this work with the following dialogue. It is not possible for me to overstate the importance of this dialogue in the time and space we constructed it, for furthering my ability to travel the path that has led to the production of this work. Dorothy Leland, my Chicana *colega*, is a person with whom I was able to travel territory that I simply could not have traveled with anyone else. We began this dialogue out of a frustration born from trying to address issues of race and racism within our own academic community. We constructed it through an exchange of e-mail messages. Thinking about the time when we engaged this dialogue, I still feel the excitement, energy, and feeling of traversing into areas new and untraveled. There were many times during the construction of this dialogue when I had to step away, feel the reverberations through my body, and come back to it when I could have access to language and writing. It is this aspect, this lived aspect of traversing borders and new territories of consciousness, that I suspect is never fully encapsulated in the writing effort. Yet traces must remain. There is something ineffable here that must be left with and in the dialogue. It is ironic and fitting that in coming to the end, with all the reflections and theorizations taken this far, we still find the dialogue as the most appropriate pausing point.

SITUATING OURSELVES IN THEORY AND PRACTICE, WITH DOROTHY LELAND

This chapter is the product of the effort of two academic feminists to explore with each other our processes of coming to consciousness as Chicana. Working through the academic context in which we share a common commitment to feminist and phenomenological work (Merleau-Ponty 1981; Bartky 1990; Young 1990), we have come to grapple with very personal issues of our own life experiences and ethnic identities. The chapter has been written in dialogue form to reflect the actual path we took in reaching our more abstract, theoretical conclusions. Through our dialogue we explore the very processes by which we come to both political and personal consciousness regarding the racism and classism that has contextualized the development of our ethnic identities.

Sharing this very personal dialogue with a larger audience seems risky. We offer up fragments of our lives as the stuff out of which theory gets made. As academics, we expect our theory and even our method to be criticized. But we must trust our audience to receive with openness the lived experiences we share; it is, after all, this recovery of lived experience that so typifies the work of radical women of color within U.S. feminist theorizing (Moraga and Anzaldúa 1983; Anzaldúa 1990).

Since the mid-1980s, the signifier "woman of color" has become a familiar inhabitant of feminist discourse. Today, there are books and essays written by self-identified "women of color." There are women-of-color caucuses, panels, and special events associated with our professional organizations. Yet it is our belief that academic feminism has not yet sufficiently explored what this signifier means—what it has been and can be constructed to represent.

In this chapter, we problematize the category "woman of color" by exploring how it has been and remains both problematical and hopeful for us. We look at how race, ethnicity, and class issues have affected our willingness to identify as "women of color" and at how these same issues affect the willingness of others to place us in that category. In the process, we explore how our assimilation into the dominant "Anglo" culture of the American Southwest reveals the racism and classism inherent in it, how our assimilation has created for us powerful barriers to assuming nonconflictual racial and ethnic identities, and how we struggle against it even as we are restrained by the racism of this culture.

DIALOGUE ON RACE, CLASS, AND CHICANA IDENTITY

DL: Like many people who live in the United States, my ethnicity is multiple and complex. I come from many peoples and countries. But the origins that are alive for me, that define and perplex me, are only two. I am the daughter of a Texan father and Mexican mother—a borderland creature, Tex-Mex.

Somewhere along the way, in the schoolyard and town in which I grew up, I learned to be white and not Mexican. I learned that Mexicans are brown—browner than me. I learned that Mexicans were those browner "others" who worked in the fields that white people owned.

Yet, even as I learned this, I traveled each summer to Mexico to visit my grandparents. My grandfather, Don Tomas, was a proud charro and businessman. But I remember him best as a storyteller. From my grandfather I inhaled rich images of his boyhood in the state of Sinaloa, growing up in a socialist colony, fleeing Mexico during the revolution in a boxcar. My grandfather wrote books about his adventures, transcribed dying native languages, and translated the diaries of Spanish explorers.

My grandmother would prepare feasts of tamales and boiled beans in honor of our visits. When she didn't want us to understand, she spoke Spanish. Daily we walked a dirt path to the local bakery, where she would buy hard-crusted rolls and pastries sprinkled with sugar. On the days we went to the meat market, I worried about the buzzing flies.

Once we visited the town of Los Mochis, where my mother was born. My grandparents chatted happily with old friends and relatives. But my mother, who was educated in the United States and spoke perfect Anglo English, seemed to have nothing to say. As we grew up, she never—not even once—talked about her childhood in Mexico. Somewhere along the way, she learned to be ashamed.

There is one more thing I need to say.

My twin brother has blond, nappy hair, and blue eyes. When he was in high school, he cut his hair short to silence the white teens who teased him about his "Afro." But I am the darkest of my siblings. My brothers and sisters sometimes used my darkness as a threat, hinting that I might not be a "real" member of the family. "You were adopted," they taunted, "a poor child abandoned on the streets of Mexico." I learned early the ostracizing, stigmatizing reality of white racism.

So, for a long time I became white and not Mexican.

JM: Like many people who live in the United States, my ethnicity is multiple and complex. I come from many peoples and countries. But I have always considered myself, first and foremost, a Californian. As a very young girl, I was always very proud of my name "Martinez." I knew it made me different—something to do with Mexico. In my childhood imagination it meant "great people," "proud warriors," "fighting spirit." I don't know where I got this, except from my father's very quiet and determined way.

But in the "real" world of people, outside of my child's imagination, my name has always, for as long as I can remember, prompted the question,

"Do you speak Spanish?" I learned that being named "Martinez" meant being "Mexican" meant speaking Spanish. Because I didn't speak Spanish I wasn't a real Mexican. I learned that Mexicans were the "low-riders" who lived in San Fernando, in the barrios, who spoke differently than I did.

My father has always been mostly silent about his life growing up. One of my most prominent memories of my father during my own childhood was his rare but impactful storytelling about the poverty within which he grew up. Short and to the point, left with no word to follow, his stories always confused me.

My grandmother was visiting us once when I was a little girl. She was making beans and tortillas for us. As she spread the beans out on the table, carefully sorting out the chunks of dirt and small rocks from the beans, my father told me how he remembered her doing that when he was a little boy, except that as the family sat around that table sorting the dirt from the beans, they looked at all the food they had for the week. As they sat around the table, my father and his brother and sister knew that that was all the food they had.

I was a little girl. We went to visit some relatives in Santa Ana, the occasion of a wedding or birthday, I think. Everyone spoke Spanish; there were all kinds of foods I didn't recognize but saw my father eat knowingly. Mexican music, dress, and decorations were all around. Years later, some unknown occasion, my father tells me how those people, my relatives in Santa Ana, used to laugh and make fun of him because his family was so poor. But after my father had moved to California, worked his way through UCLA, and earned a very good living as a corporate manager; then they invite him to their parties and celebrations. These stories told me that being poor, more than being Mexican, was the condition by which one suffered discrimination.

There was something I sensed about my father's suffering that told me that it was dangerous to ask for explanations. Both he and my grandmother: stiff-lipped, straight-backed—we didn't talk about the past. Being poor and Mexican was something we couldn't talk about. It was something hidden, dangerous, evil. I learned never to ask questions.

DL: Our stories are different, yet at important junctures so much the same. When Jackie and I talk, Chicana to Chicana, we erase silences that painfully define who we are. We discover common experiences that unite us as Mexicana, experiences that no Anglo shares. Talking Chicana to Chicana, we become more whole, more in touch with our race and ancestry.

Chicana is a consciously assumed identity. To be Chicana or Chicano, one must be Mexican American. But not all Mexican Americans are Chicana or Chicano. Identifying as Chicana or Chicano requires assuming a certain political consciousness, a resistance to being totally assimilated into Anglo culture, a commitment to bonding the surviving fragments from shared pasts into a proud and creative future. A Chicana can be light or dark skinned. But she is not white. Whiteness is a racist category that severs the Chicana from her ethnic and racial identity.

Because Anglos identify me as white, I will always have white privilege. But I grew up with the inherent contradictions of a racist-defined color spectrum inside my home and family. My blood is mixed, and my heritage defies white/nonwhite classification.

JM: Anglos identify me as white, my name an "oddity," or the sign of a Mexican family that "made it"—a Mexican that can do America proud. My father went from a childhood of extreme poverty to a life filled with the signs of middle-class white America. The more middle class he became, the less his ethnic heritage mattered, the more he could be seen as white. I've come to see how those signs of "middle class and thus white" do violence to everyone for the erasures they enact. They've done violence to my father by putting him in an either/or position. He chose *not* to have his family live the poverty he did—a decision that funneled him into whiteness and erased his own private retention of his ethnic heritage and family history of struggle and survival. My father talks about his life in terms of survival. I see how it is class, more so and differently from race, that defines my father's self-understanding.

Signs of "middle-class" achievement have done violence to me, robbing me of a space to live with my father's history. They do violence to us all by erasing my, Dorothy's, and others' ethnicity, making it easy to see us simply as white and thus works against of possibility of speaking "Chicana to Chicana."

The designator "woman of color" has been, at times, a perplexing one for me. I have been in conversations with white colleagues about the need to have more "women of color" in the academy. It seems like such discussions have the best of motivations behind them. But, I wonder, why such passion and insistence on needing women of color here when these folks are so able to erase whatever nonwhite presence I bring to these very conversations? Such moments freeze me in silence. What do I say? Do I insist that they identify me as a "woman of color" and make myself the subject of the conversation? This is a very uncomfortable thing to do—suddenly my body and my presence become the object of our discussion. Or do I simply go along and agree with this abstract commitment to "women of color" and let the erasure of my own ethnicity stand? What kind of racism gets expressed here? How do we see the need for more women of color in the academy when we are unable to see the color and difference in those who are nonwhite? I bear the signifier of the name— Hispanic, not white. Yet still, simple assumptions erase my ethnicity. I need the sign "women of color" as a designator to help create alliances in an oppositional consciousness to the power, privilege, and authority of middle-class whiteness that so dominates "America." But when this designation is taken (especially by white people) as simple and self-apparent, it reinforces the logic of racism: One is white or isn't. It is, fittingly, among my Chicana, Asian, black, and Native American colleagues that my color gains the greatest space to live.

For those of us who are not white, contradictions abound. Personal lives filled with contradictions bear struggle lived deep in the body. For those of us in the academy, we often embrace theorizing, writing, creative art—something to find expression that is not available within the received practices of a racist culture. This process is, for me, the ongoing assertation of Chicana identity.

DL: I do not (yet) know how to make art or theory from my way of being Chicana. Perhaps the identity is for me too thin—ethereal like a spirit I have not yet met.

My grandparents and mother are buried in Mexico. My cousin, Miquel, lives near the graveyard and visits with their spirits. The graves are covered with large rocks following the local Pai Pai Indian custom. When I visited the graves a few years ago, I knew that I too would be buried there. I feel a connection with the earth and rocks—some strange peace and sense of belonging.

Loss and longing to touch cultural roots define my way of being Chicana. Like Jackie, I do not speak Spanish. But I know phrases and songs—especially songs—from fragments of childhood memories. I am Chicana when I sing the songs. I am Chicana when my soul opens to bright Indian colors—vibrant yellows, oranges, reds, pinks, browns, and blues. I am Chicana when I crave a lunch of beans and corn tortillas.

Perhaps the loss and longing is for my mother, who slowly went mad as I grew up. Anglo medicine said that she was paranoid schizophrenic; she said she was possessed. Sometimes she assumed separate identities as a saint and as a devil. Her saint name was Maria, her devil name Mr. Underwood.

I remember a psychiatrist commenting on the Mr. Underwood name— the Underwood deviled ham product with the pitchforked devil logo its obvious source. Only recently have I wondered about the devil's gender and the saint name, the equally obvious Maria.

Jackie, Chicana to Chicana, I'll tell you one more story. Before my mother died, she underwent a ritual exorcism, arranged by family in southern California. I was here, in Indiana, but promised to observe the hours of the ritual sitting in silence. I lit a candle and listened to a recording of Mozart's Requiem.

Later my brother told me that during the exorcism there was a good spirit in the room; he believed the spirit was me. I don't believe in spirits, good or bad. I am far too Anglo and modern European for that. But I am comforted by the cheap plastic statues that ward off snakes and other ominous things by the grave where my mother is buried.

In this comfort—in affirming it—I am also Chicana.

JM: Dorothy, mi amiga, Chicana to Chicana, we speak from places of such pain, loss and longing, perplexity, danger, and possibility. As I live with your words and hear my own—for the first time, in a way, because of their nearness to yours—I feel a familiar kindling deep inside that I have learned to walk away from.

It's a kindling that was first nourished by my grandmother on my mother's mostly Anglo side. But I have American Indian heritage on my mother's side as well. I grew up hearing stories about how my grandfather's great-grandmother was a pure-blood Tennessee Cherokee. My grandfather knew this, as the story goes, because oil was found on a reservation there and my grandfather's family had a genealogy done to find out if they were entitled to any of it.

My grandmother was a deeply spiritual woman, and though she often evoked the name of Jesus Christ, she was spiritual in a no-man kind of way. I never associated her spirituality with church or buildings or the image of Christ crucified. I associated her spirituality with the desert—incomprehensibly beautiful, the Earth, the magic of a desert sunset. After dinner, walking with my grandmother, holding her hand as she swung her arms vigorously in front and behind her shouting for all the Earth and sky to hear "Oh, Joy, Oh Joy, Oh Joy" in a continuous refrain.

My grandmother has always known that I'm an Indian. I grew up, it seems, telling her stories about my past life as an Indian. She knew my stories to be true, and she always nurtured my belief in a spirit world that lives in the Earth and sky, far beyond this ordinary world we live in. Though I have no recollection of telling my grandmother these stories, the spirit world that she helped me to live in has always been so very real for me; the desert a deeply spiritual place.

But I haven't been able too spend much time living in that world. I learned that my Indian wasn't a real Indian. I learned that there could be no connection between my "ethnicity" and those old stories I used to tell my grandmother. I learned that there was no connection between the fact of my name, which I got from my father, and the fact of the Indian spirituality I got from my maternal grandmother.

Throughout my life, I've felt only tiny prods, here and there, kindlings that spark deep within my feeling-spirit. I felt it when I first joined the Chicano Student Organization at California State, Northridge. I felt it when I attended the National Association of Chicano Studies meeting and felt overwhelmed with warmth and senses of possibility as I spent those days roaming among rooms full of brown women and men talking about this brownness, whiteness, struggle, and racism. I felt it as I sat in the audience and listened to Joy Harjo read her poetry about the native people, their struggles and then as I spoke with her afterward and she asked me about my life, where I'm from, the Indian in me—a connection so deep that I could only barely stumble out a few words, taken as I was by her seeing Indian in me.

These tiny prods here and there, as this speaking with you, Chicana to Chicana, are joy for me. They contain an incredible sense of possibility. But they are also much more than joy and possibility. They are also laced with danger, serious danger, paralyzing danger.

I came to the academy so that I could live those parts of me that have been erased. All of my studies, my reading, writing, and speaking, are part of that effort to live and become that which has been silenced in my life. This is not an abstract effort—it is a concrete effort of struggle that I engage every day.

I've always been a theoretician, beginning in those very early days when my father's stories gave me great pause; theorizing has always been about figuring things out, about understanding, discovery, and possibility. As I grew up, my discovery of my lesbianism became the most pressing site of conscious struggle. I understood the profundity of cultural erasure most obviously here. Realizing that I was a lesbian led me to understand how that knowledge about myself was hidden by cultural biases that gave me no way to understand feelings that I had always had. Through this struggle I came also to understand the erasures and hidden presences of my ethnic heritage and thus came to see the common ways in which cultural norms can rob us of who we are.

Now that I'm in the academy, I can read and write "as a Chicana," but that is fraught with just as many dangers. I haven't felt smart enough about racism and my own life and heritage to be able to outsmart the racisms at work. I've been tokenized for my name, served the interests of white racism.

DL: I came to the academy to escape from the small town where I grew up. I still hate that place, so full of mean-spirited prejudice and sick bigotry. This town was one of the first in the United States to declare English as its "official" language—a blatant effort to rob the large Mexican immigrant population of even the semblance of democratic right.

When I entered the academy, I never declared myself as "Hispanic" on those forms in which institutions attempt to quantify the ethnic and racial mix of their student population. At first, this was because I recognized myself only as white. But as I learned to see through race and class stereotypes and the deeply hidden fears I had of being discovered as Mexican, my motivation changed. As I filled out those forms, I would say to myself, "You do not get to count me. That would be too easy. I do not embody the differences you fear."

I viewed this as a small attempt to thwart the interests of white racism. I'm not the sort of Hispanic who makes Anglos uncomfortable: I have neither the stereotypical name or look. Lately I've adopted a somewhat different strategy: Now I check both the "white" and "Hispanic" boxes, even though you are supposed to declare yourself as only one. It is a little protest against the logic of racism, which says "you must be either one or the other"—which recognizes only blood that is pure.

I have similar problems with the signifier "woman of color." Jackie, you claim it as an oppositional space from out of which to speak. But I feel fraudulent assuming this identity. I'll try to explain why.

I have white-skin privilege by virtue of the fact that the dominant culture does not identify me as "being colored." "Color" is a signifier of visibility—of a presumed otherness and inferiority based on how one looks. No matter what my actual skin shade, if my skin, or facial features, or speech patterns fail to mark me as being "of color," I do not suffer in the eyes of the dominant culture the stigma of that mark.

When the signifier "women of color" first emerged in feminist circles, it was used to designate a vast and undifferentiated arena of "otherness." African Americans, Asian Americans, Hispanic Americans, Native Americans, and so on were lumped together as "women of color." But this categorization simply replicates the extant racist white/colored dichotomy. Today, "people of color" still signifies "people who are black" to most North Americans. Since I have not borne the stigma of "being colored" in white eyes, it feels fraudulent to attempt to claim the oppositional space, "women of color," as my own.

But neither am I white if being white means not being Chicana.

I'm talking about what Cherríe Moraga calls the "whitewash of cultural identity." Cherríe, who grew up in a town fifteen miles northwest of the community where I was Anglicized, explains, "No one ever quite told me this (that light is right), but I knew that being light was something valued in my family (who were all Chicano, with the exception of my father.) In fact, everything about my upbringing . . . attempted to bleach me of what color I did have."

So, Jackie, this is what I've been trying to say. Like Cherríe, I am a woman best described as "one who has been bleached." And like most bleached women, when I am lucky, blotches of brown bleed through.

JM: Feeling fraudulent. I've felt that all my life, beginning with the question, "Do you speak Spanish?" Interesting how that question came mostly from white people. Interesting how the places I've felt most fraudulent is among white people. Interesting how in the Chicano Studies

Department at UCSB I was welcomed, my difference from others not used to mark me as fraudulent. Interesting how my students there, just like the ones at the East Coast Chicano Students Association's annual Pachanga, looked to me for advice about being a Chicana in the academy, advice about how they might pursue their own life. Interesting how in conversations with my Chicana friends my identity as Chicana is simply taken as a basis on which we come to understand our similarities and differences so as to engage a common struggle.

DL: Among Chicanas, there is greater recognition of our differences. Some of us are gay; some of us are not. Some of us come from the haciendados and merchant classes; some of us have only worked the land of others. Some of us are more European; some of us more Mayan or mestizo. We have dark and light skins; blond and black hair, short and tall statures.

Anglo culture tends to construct all Mexicans as being "the same." Where I grew up, being Mexican meant being poor, brown, and ignorant. The migrants who journeyed north to pick fruit and work the fields had different ways: They lived in shacks, their children went without shoes, they spoke a language that signified their lack of education and stupidity.

Escaping poverty required becoming Anglicized, whited. Only good English would allow you to become something other than a "stupid Mexican." Wearing Anglo suits, adopting Anglo customs, living in Anglo homes: These were/are signs of one's escape from being a dark blot on a white cultural landscape.

Many Anglos do not realize that Mexico is a class- and race-stratified society. The less Indian, the more European, the more wealth: the better. This racist and classist heritage travels across borders, creating powerful internal pressures to adopt the garb, customs, and speech of white middle-class America. This pressure has affected all Mexican Americans despite our race and class differences. It forms a common locus of Chicana experience and resistance.

I have never known the extreme poverty of many of my Chicana sisters. The fact that we—my family—were not braceros but haciendados is a difference that cannot be overlooked. But this difference is one between Chicanas and hence presupposes other experiences that we share. Class like skin color does not make Chicanas invisible to other Chicanas.

JM: My father felt his identity most poignantly as poor, dirt poor. He came to achieve all of the signs of middle class. I've worked hard to understand my father's life. In brief conversations here and there, almost always stilted, full of hesitancy of both sides—I've come to understand that his achievement of "Anglo" markers has been in an absolutely dedicated effort to be faithful to *la familia*. Not an assimilator or a cop-out on his race but a testament to the power and dignity of people who are ostracized for being poor. He proved himself better. But in a society where racism and classism are twin brothers, his very success economically has meant the erasure of this ethnicity. My father's very life can be seen as an example of how racism and classism are intertwined. Because he aspired to provide for his family what he did not have in his birth family, Anglo culture could recognize him only in its own racist terms. To succumb to a single trajectory in understanding how people are positioned by race, class, gender, or sexuality is to reinscribe those very oppressions we are trying to subvert. This is the lesson I am learning.

CONCLUSION

At the beginning of this chapter, we promised to problematize the category "woman of color" by exploring how it has been and remains problematical for us. We hope that we have succeeded in this.

Both of us were born *la güera*: fair skinned. This physiognomic trait has shaped our experience both inside and outside Anglo and Chicana communities. But the trait itself would not have assumed for us or others the significance it has outside of a racist culture. Being fair skinned has enabled us to reap the benefits of white privilege. But passing or being labeled by others as white has also meant ethnic invisibility. This is because Anglo culture has constructed "Mexican" as a homogeneous group— as those brown-skinned "beaners," "wetbacks," and "spicks."

For both of us, identifying as Chicana has meant resisting total assimilation into Anglo culture and whiteness. This identification is a political act, an interruption of the bleaching process that attempts to launder out mestizo blood and spirit, as if it were an ominous stain on an otherwise superior cloth of white/Anglo identity. Thus, when our Anglo feminist friends identify us as white, we simultaneously understand and resist. We understand that we share the privileges accorded to fair-skinned persons in a racist culture. But we resist because the sense in which they are white and we are white is profoundly different. Anglos do not become white through a process of bleaching: Their being seen and treated as white does not entail an erasure of cultural roots and ethnic identities.

BIBLIOGRAPHY

Acuña, Rodolfo. 1988. *Occupied America: A History of Chicanos.* 3rd ed. New York: HarperCollins.

Alarcón, Norma. 1983. "Chicana's Feminist Literature: A Re-Vision through Malintzin/or Malintzin: Putting Flesh Back on the Object." In *This Bridge Called My Back: Writings by Radical Women of Color,* edited by Cherríe Moraga and Gloria Anzaldúa. New York: Kitchen Table: Women of Color Press.

———. 1990. "The Theoretical Subject(s) of This Bridge Called My Back and Anglo-American Feminism." In *Making Face, Making Soul/Haciendo Caras: Creative and Critical Perspectives by Women of Color,* edited by Gloria Anzaldúa. San Francisco: Aunt Lute Foundation.

Alarcón, Norma, et al., eds. 1993. *Chicana Critical Issues.* Series in Chicana/Latina Studies. Berkeley, Calif.: Third Woman Press.

Alcoff, Linda. 1992. "The Problem of Speaking for Others." *Cultural Critique* 20: 5–32.

Allen, Jeffner. 1983. "Through the Wild Region: An Essay in Phenomenological Feminism." *Review of Existential Psychology and Psychiatry* 18, nos. 1–3: 241–256.

Allen, Jeffner, and Iris Marion Young, eds. 1989. *The Thinking Muse: Feminism and Modern French Philosophy.* Bloomington: Indiana University Press.

Allen, Paula Gunn. 1992. *The Sacred Hoop: Recovering the Feminine in American Indian Traditions.* Reprint, Boston: Beacon Press, 1986.

Anzaldúa, Gloria. 1987. *Borderlands/La Frontera: The New Mestiza.* San Francisco: Aunt Lute Foundation.

———, ed. 1990. *Making Face, Making Soul/Haciendo Caras: Creative and Critical Perspectives by Women of Color.* San Francisco: Aunt Lute Foundation.

Baca Zinn, M., L. Weber Cannon, E. Higginbotham, and B. Thornton Dill. 1986. "The Costs of Exclusionary Practices in Women's Studies." *Signs: Journal of Women in Culture and Society* 11, no. 21: 290–303.

Bar On, Bat Ami. 1993. "Marginality and Epistemic Privilege." In *Feminist Epistemologies,* edited by Linda Alcoff and Elizabeth Potter. New York: Routledge.

Barrera, Martha. 1991. "Café con Leche." In *Chicana Lesbians: The Girls Our Mothers Warned Us About,* edited by Carla Trujillo. Berkeley, Calif.: Third Woman Press.

Bartky, S. L. 1990. *Femininity and Domination. Studies in the Phenomenology of Oppression.* New York: Routledge.

Bateson, Gregory. 1972. *Steps to an Ecology of Mind.* New York: Ballantine Books.

Blackwood, Evelyn. 1984. "Sexuality and Gender in Certain Native American Tribes: The Case of Cross-Gender Females." *Signs: Journal of Women in Culture and Society* 10: 27–42.

Bordieu, Pierre. 1977. *Outline of a Theory of Practice.* Cambridge Studies in Anthropology. Translated by Richard Nice. Reprint, Cambridge: Cambridge University Press, 1972.

Broyles, Yolanda J. 1990. "Women in El Teatro Campensino: '¿Apoco Estaba Molacha La Virgen de Guadalupe?'" In *Chicana Voices: Intersections of Class, Race, and Gender,* edited by Teresa Córdova, Norma Cantú, Gilberto Cardenas, Juan García, and Christine M. Sierra. Reprint, Austin, Tex.: University of Austin, Center for Mexican American Studies/National Association of Chicano Studies, 1986.

Butler, Judith. 1986. "Sex and Gender in Simone de Beauvoir's *Second Sex.*" *Yale French Studies* 72: 35–49.

———. 1989. "Sexual Ideology and Phenomenological Description: A Feminist Critique of Merleau-Ponty's *Phenomenology of Perception.*" In *The Thinking Muse: Feminism and Modern French Philosophy,* edited by Jeffner Allen and Iris Marion Young. Bloomington: Indiana University Press.

———. 1990. "Performative Acts and Gender Constitution: An Essay in Phenomenology and Feminist Theory." In *Performing Feminisms: Feminist Critical Theory and Theatre,* edited by Sue-Ellen Case. Baltimore: The Johns Hopkins University Press.

———. 1993. *Bodies That Matter: On the Discursive Limits of "Sex."* New York: Routledge.

Castañeda, Antonia I. 1993. "Sexual Violence in the Politics and Policies of Conquest: Amerindian Women and the Spanish Conquest of Alta California." In *Building with Our Hands: New Directions in Chicana Studies,* edited by Adela de la Torre and Beatríz M. Pesquera. Berkeley and Los Angeles: University of California Press.

Castillo, Ana. 1994. *Massacre of the Dreamers: Essays on Xicanisma.* Albuquerque: University of New Mexico Press.

Cisneros, Sandra. 1998. "A Woman of No Consequence Una Mujer Cualquiera." In *Living Chicana Theory,* edited by Carla Trujillo. Berkeley, Calif.: Third Woman Press.

Córdova, Teresa. 1994. "Roots and Resistance: The Emergent Writings of Twenty Years of Chicana Feminist Struggle." In *Handbook of Hispanic Cultures in the Unites States: Sociology,* edited by Félix Padilla. Houston: Arte Publico Press.

Cott, Nancy. 1987. *The Grounding of Modern Feminism.* New Haven, Conn.: Yale University Press.

Cypress, Sandra M. 1991. *La Malinche in Mexican Literature: From History to Myth.* Austin: University of Texas Press.

Darder, Antonia, ed. 1995. *Culture and Difference: Critical Perspectives on the Bicultural Experience in the United States.* Westport, Conn.: Bergin and Garvey.

Davis, Angela Y. 1990. *Women, Culture, and Politics.* Reprint, New York: Vintage Books, 1984.

De Beauvoir, Simone. 1989. *The Second Sex.* Translated and edited by H. M. Parshley. Reprint, New York: Vintage Books, 1952.

De la Torre, Adela, and Beatríz M. Pesquera. 1993. *Building with Our Hands: New Directions in Chicana Studies.* Berkeley and Los Angeles: University of California Press.

De Lauretis, Teresa. 1984. *Alice Doesn't: Feminism, Semiotics, Cinema.* Bloomington: Indiana University Press.

———. 1987. *Technologies of Gender: Essays on Theory, Film, and Fiction.* Bloomington: Indiana University Press.

Faderman, Lillian. 1981. *Surpassing the Love of Men: Romantic Friendship and Love between Women from the Renaissance to the Present.* New York: William Morrow.

Fanon, Frantz. 1967. *Black Skin, White Masks.* New York: Grove Press.

Foucault, Michel. 1970. *The Order of Things: An Archaeology of the Human Sciences.* New York: Vintage Books.

———. 1972a. *The Archaeology of Knowledge and the Discourse on Language.* New York: Pantheon Books.

———. 1972b. "History, Discourse and Discontinuity." *Salmagundi* 20: 225–248.

———. 1980. *The History of Sexuality, Volume I.* New York: Vintage Books.

Fuss, Diana. 1989. *Essentially Speaking: Feminism, Nature, and Difference.* New York: Routledge.

Galindo, Letticia, and María Gonzales, eds. 1999. *Speaking Chicana: Voice, Power and Identity.* Tucson: University of Arizona Press.

García, Alma M. 1989. "The Development of Chicana Feminist Discourse, 1970–1980." *Gender & Society* 3: 217–238.

———. 1997, ed. *Chicana Feminist Thought: The Basic Historical Writings.* New York: Routledge.

Giddings, Paula. 1984. *When and Where I Enter: The Impact of Black Women on Race and Sex in America.* New York: Bantam Books.

Goldberg, David Theo. 1993. *Racist Culture: Philosophy and the Politics of Meaning.* London and New York: Basil Blackwell.

Gonzales, Sylvia. 1977. "The White Feminist Movement: The Chicana Perspective." *The Social Science Journal* 14, no. 3: 67–76.

González, Deena J. 1993. "La Tules of Image and Reality: Euro-American Attitudes and Legend Formation on a Spanish-Mexican Frontier." In *Building with Our Hands: New Directions in Chicana Studies*, edited by Adela de la Torre and Beatríz M. Pesquera. Berkeley and Los Angeles: University of California Press.

González, Maria C. 2000. "De/Reconstructing the Mother from the Shadows of Mexican Womanhood: Performing an Embodied Rosary." Dissertation, University of Creation Spirituality, Oakland, California.

Gordon, Lewis. 1995. *Bad Faith and Antiblack Racism.* Atlantic Highlands, N.J.: Humanities Press.

————. 1997. *Her Majesty's Other Children: Sketches of Racism from a Neo-colonial Age.* Lanham, Md.: Rowman and Littlefield.

Guy-Sheftall, Beverly, ed. 1995. *Words of Fire: An Anthology of African American Feminist Thought.* New York: The New Press.

Harding, Sandra. 1986. *The Science Question in Feminism.* Ithaca, N.Y.: Cornell University Press.

————. 1991. *Whose Science? Whose Knowledge? Thinking from Women's Lives.* Ithaca, N.Y.: Cornell University Press.

Hartsock, N. 1983. "The Feminist Standpoint: Developing the Ground for a Specifically Feminist Historical Materialism." In *Discovering Reality: Feminist Perspectives on Epistemology, Metaphysics, Methodology, and Philosophy of Science,* edited by S. Harding and M. B. Hintikka. Dordrecht: D. Reidel Publishing.

Hererra-Sobek, María, and Helena María Viramontes, eds. 1988. *Chicana Creativity and Criticism: Charting New Frontiers in American Literature.* Houston: Arte Publico Press/University of Houston.

Hernández-Ávila, I. 1997. "An Open Letter to Chicanas: On the Power and Politics of Origin." In *Reinventing the Enemy's Language: Contemporary Native Women's Writings of North America,* edited by Joy Harjo and Gloria Bird. New York: W. W. Norton.

Hill Collins, Patricia. 1986. "Learning from the Outsider Within: The Sociological Significance of Black Feminist Thought." *Social Problems* 33, no. 6: S14–S32.

High, Freida. 1997. "Chiasmus—Art in Politics/Politics in Art: Chicano/a and African American Image, Text, and Activism of the 1960s and 1970s." In *Voices of Color: Art and Society in the Americas,* edited by Phoebe Farris-Dufrene. Atlantic Highlands, N.J.: Humanities Press.

hooks, bell. 1990. *Yearning: Race, Gender, and Cultural Politics.* Boston: South End Press.

Ihde, Don. 1986. *Experimental Phenomenology: An Introduction.* Albany: State University of New York Press.

Langellier, Kristin M. 1989. "Personal Narratives: Perspectives on Theory and Research." *Text and Performance Quarterly* 9, no. 4: 243–276.

————. 1994. "Appreciating Phenomenology and Feminism: Researching Quiltmaking and Communication." *Human Studies* 17: 65–80.

Lanigan, Richard L. 1988. *Phenomenology of Communication: Merleau-Ponty's Thematics in Communicology and Semiology.* Pittsburgh: Duquesne University Press.

————. 1991. *Speaking and Semiology: Maurice Merleau-Ponty's Phenomenological Theory of Existential Communication.* Reprint, Berlin: Mouton de Gruyter, 1972.

————. 1992. *The Human Science of Communicology: A Phenomenology of Discourse in Foucault and Merleau-Ponty.* Pittsburgh: Duquesne University Press.

Las Casas, Bartolomé. 1992. *In Defense of the Indians.* Translated and edited by Stafford Poole. Reprint, DeKalb: Northern Illinois University Press, 1552.

Leon-Portilla, Miguel. 1992. *The Broken Spears: The Aztec Account of the Conquest of Mexico.* Reprint, Boston: Beacon Press, 1962.

López, Tiffany Ana, ed. 1993. *Growing up Chicana/o.* New York: Avon Books.

Lorde, Audre. 1984. *Sister Outsider: Essays and Speeches.* Trumansburg, N.Y.: The Crossing Press.

Lugones, María. 1987. "Playfulness, 'World'-Travelling, and Loving Perception." In *Making Face, Making Soul: Haciendo Caras,* edited by Gloria Anzaldúa. San Francisco: Aunt Lute Foundation.

MacKinnon, Catharine A. 1987. *Feminism Unmodified: Discourses on Life and Law.* Cambridge, Mass.: Harvard University Press.

McFeat, Tom. 1974. *Small-Group Cultures.* New York: Pergamon Press.

Mendoza-Denton, Norma. 1999. "Fighting Words: Latina Girls, Gangs, and Language Attitudes." In *Speaking Chicana: Voice, Power, and Identity,* edited by Letticia Galindo and María Dolores Gonzales. Tucson: University of Arizona Press.

Mercer, Kobena. 1993. "Looking for Trouble." In *The Lesbian and Gay Studies Reader,* edited by Henry Abelove, Michèle Ania Barale, and David M. Halperin. New York: Routledge.

Merleau-Ponty, Maurice. 1964. *Signs.* Evanston, Ill.: Northwestern University Press.

———. 1986. *Phenomenology of Perception.* Translated by Colin Smith (with revisions by Forrest Williams and David Guerrière). Reprint, Atlantic Highlands, N.J.: Humanities Press, 1962.

Merrell, Floyd. 1995. *Peirce's Semiotics Now: A Primer.* Toronto: Canadian Scholar's Press.

Mirandé, Alfredo, and Evangelina Enríquez. 1979. *La Chicana: The Mexican-American Woman.* Chicago: University of Chicago Press.

Mohanty, Chandra Talpade, Ann Russo, and Lourdes Torres, eds. 1991. *Third World Women and the Politics of Feminism.* Bloomington: Indiana University Press.

Moraga, Cherríe. 1981. "La Güera." In *This Bridge Called My Back: Writings by Radical Women of Color,* edited by Cherríe Moraga and Gloria Anzaldúa. New York: Kitchen Table: Women of Color Press.

———. 1983. *Loving in the War Years: Lo Que Nunca Pasó Por Sus Labios.* Boston: South End Press.

———. 1993. *The Last Generation: Poetry and Prose.* Boston: South End Press.

Moraga, Cherríe, and Gloria Anzaldúa, eds. 1983. *This Bridge Called My Back: Writings by Radical Women of Color.* New York: Kitchen Table: Women of Color Press.

Muñoz, Carlos, Jr. 1989. *Youth, Identity, Power: The Chicano Movement.* New York: Verso.

Orozco, Aurora. 1999. "Mexican Blood Runs through My Veins." In *Speaking Chicana: Voice, Power, and Identity,* edited by Letticia Galindo and María Dolores Gonzales. Tucson: University of Arizona Press.

Peirce, Charles Sanders. 1958. *The Collected Papers of Charles Sanders Peirce.* 8 vols. Edited by Charles Hartshorne, Paul Weiss, and Arthur Burks. Cambridge, Mass.: Harvard University Press.

Pérez, Emma. 1991. "Gulf Dreams," In *Chicana Lesbians: The Girls Our Mothers Warned Us About,* edited by Carla Trujillo. Berkeley, Calif.: Third Woman Press.

Ramos, Juanita, ed. 1987. *Compañeras: Latina Lesbians.* New York: Latina Lesbian Herstory Project.

Rebolledo, Tey D., and Eliana S. Rivero. 1983. *Infinite Divisions: An Anthology of Chicana Literature.* Tucson: University of Arizona Press.

Reusch, Jurgen, and Gregory Bateson 1987. *Communication: The Social Matrix of Psychiatry.* Reprint, New York: W. W. Norton, 1951.

Rich, Adrienne. 1993. "Compulsory Heterosexuality and Lesbian Existence." In *The Lesbian and Gay Studies Reader,* edited by Henry Abelove, Michèle Ania Barale, and David M. Halperin. Reprint, New York: Routledge, 1982.

Rodriguez, Richard. 1982. *Hunger of Memory: The Education of Richard Rodriguez.* New York: Bantam Books.

Ruiz, Vicki L. 1993. "'Star Struck': Acculturation, Adolescence, and the Mexican American Woman, 1920–1950." In *Building with Our Hands: New Directions in Chicana Studies,* edited by Adela De la Torre and Beatríz M. Pesquera. Berkeley and Los Angeles: University of California Press.

Sánchez, Marta Ester. 1985. *Contemporary Chicana Poetry: A Critical Approach to an Emerging Literature.* Berkeley and Los Angeles: University of California Press.

Sandoval, Chela. 1991. "U.S. Third World Feminism: The Theory and Method of Oppositional Consciousness in the Postmodern World." *Genders* 10: 1–24.

———. 1995. "New Sciences: Cyborg Feminist and the Methodology of the Oppressed." In *The Cyborg Handbook,* edited by Chris Gray. New York: Routledge.

———. 1998. "Mestizaje as Method: Feminists-of-Color Challenge the Canon." In *Living Chicana Theory,* edited by Carla Trujillo. Berkeley, Calif.: Third Woman Press.

Schrag, Calvin O. 1986. *Communicative Praxis and the Space of Subjectivity.* Bloomington: Indiana University Press.

Sedgwick, Eve Kosofsky. 1990. *Epistemology of the Closet.* Berkeley and Los Angeles: University of California Press.

Sobchack, Vivian. 1992. *The Address of the Eye: A Phenomenology of Film Experience.* Princeton, N.J.: Princeton University Press.

Spitzack, Carole. 1988. "The Confession Mirror: Plastic Images for Surgery." *Canadian Journal of Political and Social Theory* 12, nos. 1–2: 38–50.

Spivak, Gayatri C. 1988. "Subaltern Studies: Deconstructing Historiography." In *Other Worlds: Essays in Cultural Politics.* New York: Routledge.

Takaki, Ronald. 1993. *A Different Mirror: A History of Multicultural America.* Boston: Little, Brown.

Todorov, Tsvetan. 1992. *The Conquest of America: The Question of the Other.* Translated by Richard Howard. Reprint, New York: Harper Perennial, 1982.

Trujillo, Carla, ed. 1991. *Chicana Lesbians: The Girls Our Mothers Warned Us About.* Berkeley, Calif.: Third Woman Press.

———, ed. 1998. *Living Chicana Theory.* Berkeley, Calif.: Third Woman Press.

Yarbro-Bejarano, Yvonne. 1990. "The Female Subject in Chicano Theatre: Sexuality, 'Race,' and Class." In *Performing Feminisms: Feminist Critical Theory and Theatre,* edited by Sue Ellen Case. Baltimore: The Johns Hopkins University Press.

Young, I. M. 1984. "Pregnant Embodiment: Subjectivity and Alienation." *Journal of Medicine and Philosophy* 9: 45–62.

———. 1990. *Throwing Like a Girl and Other Essays in Feminist Philosophy and Social Theory.* Bloomington: Indiana University Press.

Zavella, Patricia. 1987. *Women's Work and Chicano Families: Cannery Workers of the Santa Clara Valley.* Ithaca, N.Y.: Cornell University Press.

INDEX

ABOUT THE AUTHOR

Jacqueline M. Martinez received her Associate of Arts degree from Los Angeles Pierce College, her Bachelor of Arts degree from California State University at Northridge, and her Master of Science and Doctor of Philosophy degrees from Southern Illinois University. She has taught at the University of California at Santa Barbara, where she was a Chicana Dissertation Fellow; at Babson College in Wellesley, Massachusetts; and at Purdue University. She currently teaches in the Hugh Downs School of Human Communication at Arizona State University. She also holds the rank sandan (third-degree black belt) in traditional Shotokan karate-do.